THE *Middle East* COLLECTION

THE *Middle East* COLLECTION

The Palace School of
Muhammad the Conqueror

BY

BARNETTE MILLER

ARNO PRESS
A New York Times Company
New York—1973

Reprint Edition 1973 by Arno Press Inc.

Copyright, 1941, by The President and Fellows
 of Harvard College
Reprinted by permission of Harvard University
 Press

Reprinted from a copy in
 The University of Illinois Library

The Middle East Collection
ISBN for complete set: 0-405-05310-X
See last pages of this volume for titles.

Manufactured in the United States of America

———◆———

Library of Congress Cataloging in Publication Data

Miller, Barnette.
    The Palace School of Muhammad the Conqueror.

    (The Middle East collection)
    Reprint of the ed. published by Harvard University
Press, Cambridge, Mass., which was issued as no. 17 of
Harvard historical monographs.
    Forms the second volume of a trilogy on the Grand
seraglio of Stambul. The first volume, Beyond the
sublime porte, was published in 1931.
    Includes bibliographical references.
    1. Istanbul Seraglio. Palace school. I. Title.
II. Series. III. Series: Harvard historical
monographs, 17.
LF5321.I7S454 1973   371.9'62'094961   73-6291
ISBN 0-405-05349-5

HARVARD HISTORICAL MONOGRAPHS

XVII

PUBLISHED UNDER THE DIRECTION OF THE DEPARTMENT
OF HISTORY FROM THE INCOME OF

THE ROBERT LOUIS STROOCK FUND

LONDON : HUMPHREY MILFORD

OXFORD UNIVERSITY PRESS

The Palace School of Muhammad the Conqueror

BY

BARNETTE MILLER

Professor of History, Wellesley College

Cambridge

HARVARD UNIVERSITY PRESS

MCMXLI

To my Turkish Students

OF

Istanbul Woman's College

PREFACE

The Palace School of Muhammad the Conqueror forms the second volume of a trilogy on the Grand Seraglio of Stambul (*Top Qapu Sarayi*), the residence of the Turkish sultans and the seat of the Sublime Porte for nearly four centuries. The first volume of this trilogy, *Beyond the Sublime Porte*, a general history and description of the institutions and activities of the Grand Seraglio, was published by the Yale University Press in 1931. The third volume, which is in process of preparation, is a study of the political influence of the royal harem. The present monograph is a history of the training school for government officials, military officers, and court functionaries which was established by Muhammad II and which was undoubtedly one of his most important creations.

The main sources for this monograph have been records by the students of the school, both European and Turkish, contemporary diplomatic reports, contemporary books of travel and memoirs, contemporary studies of Turkish polity, and the history of the school, *Tarikhi Ata*, by the modern Turkish historian, Tayyar Zadeh Mehmed Ata Bey, references to all of which are fully given in the Notes, appended at the end of this volume.

In addition to the numerous acknowledgments already made in the preface to *Beyond the Sublime Porte*, especially for the assistance of my Turkish students and of Feridun Bey in the translation of Turkish texts,

I wish to express my gratitude to Dr. George C. Miles of the Department of Oriental Languages and Literatures of Princeton University for a careful checking of the transliteration of Turkish and Arabic words; to Miss Helen J. Sleeper, Research Librarian in Music of Wellesley College, for suggestions in regard to the section on Turkish music in Chapter IV; to Professor Duncan Black Macdonald of Hartford Theological Seminary and Mrs. Ruth Stellhorn Mackensen for their generous aid in the identification of the various Arabic works alluded to in Chapter IV; to Miss Agnes F. Perkins, my friend and colleague at Istanbul Woman's College and at Wellesley College, for her untiring assistance in the editing of my manuscript; and to Professor Albert Howe Lybyer, Chairman of the Department of History of the University of Illinois, and to Professor William Leonard Langer, Coolidge Professor of History of Harvard University, for reading the manuscript and for valuable suggestions in regard to it. The courtesy of the Princeton University Press has made possible the reprinting of Chapter IV, which first appeared in *The Macdonald Presentation Volume* (Princeton University Press, 1933). In particular I desire to express my great indebtedness to the Department of History of Harvard University for the inclusion of this volume in the Harvard Historical Monographs.

B. M.

WELLESLEY COLLEGE
April 5, 1941

CONTENTS

ILLUSTRATIONS

THE PALACE SCHOOL OF
MUHAMMAD THE CONQUEROR

Ce ne sont pas ces magnificences qui rendent celui [Grand Seraglio] de notre Empereur si renommé; ses bâtiments sont solides sans ordre d'architecture; ses meubles riches sans ajustement, et ses jardins spacieux et rustiques sans ornement; mais sa beauté principale consiste dans l'ordre que l'on y observe, et l'éducation de ceux lesquels sont destinés au service des puissances qui l'habitent. — Pétis de La Croix: *État général de l'Empire Ottoman* (1695), I, 342

INTRODUCTION

THE knowledge of the Turks which has existed in the Occident until recently has been very limited. It has been confined almost wholly to their past military glory, the fanatical aspect of their religion, a magnificence so great that Europeans — not Turks — bestowed the epithet of "Magnificent" upon Suleiman in the magnificent age of the Renaissance, and certain sensational features such as massacres and the harem system — generally viewed through the perspective of the Crusades and the modern Protestant missionary movement. As a consequence the Turkish nation has for centuries been viewed with an ignorant prejudice almost unparalleled in history. There has been little or no recognition or understanding of such laudable features of its history as the phenomenal rapidity of its rise and growth, the ability of the sultans and of the ruling class in general during the period when the empire was at its height, the high degree of organization and the interest of some of its institutions, and the staying power which has enabled the nation to survive the natural period of decline and the machinations and intrigues of the great powers over a period of more than three centuries. The amazing resurgence of the Turks in the republic of to-day calls for a more comprehensive knowledge and a more judicial view of their history.

One of the most remarkable of their institutions and at the same time one of the most remarkable educational institutions of its time, indeed of any time, was the

Palace School (*Enderun*) or great military school of state of the Grand Seraglio, founded by Muhammad the Conqueror shortly after the conquest of Constantinople and continued by his successors until the reign of Mahmud II in the first quarter of the nineteenth century The training covered an average period of about twelve to fourteen years and combined in almost equal proportions instruction in the humanities of Islam, in physical training and the arts of war and government, and in manual training; it was one of the most formal, systematic, and arduous courses ever devised in preparation for a public career. As the keystone of the Turkish polity and one of the prime factors which carried the Ottoman Empire to its full flowering and helped to stay its decline by the strength of the traditions which were centered there, the importance of this school can hardly be overestimated. When the leadership of the early sultans had come to an end, it was the momentum gathered in this school which served, perhaps more than any other single force, to extend the life of the moribund empire far beyond its natural term.

Apart from the lack of interest in Turkish history in general and the difficulties of the Turkish language, the chief explanation of the absence of knowledge of the Palace School is the heavy veil of secrecy which surrounded everything lying beyond the third gate of the Grand Seraglio, the Gate of Felicity, which was the dividing line between the Inner Palace, or House of Felicity, and the Outer Palace and the world beyond it. The women of the royal harem and the eunuchs were immured for life within the House of Felicity, and the pages for the entire period of their study. Upon leav-

ing it, the pages were bound by a vow of secrecy, be-
trayal of which meant ruin and death. The high stakes
at issue and the heavy penalties were, for the most part,
sufficient to keep them faithful to their vows. Under
an absolute despotism it is not surprising, therefore,
that information left by those who remained in the
Turkish service either is nonexistent, or else belongs to
the later period when the discipline of the school was
relaxed.

Although the educational aspect of the Palace School
has been largely lost sight of, contemporary writers bear
witness to the substantial nature of the instruction given
there and the importance of the school in Turkish polity.
Paolo Giovio, Bishop of Nocera, writing in 1538 of the
pages of the Palace School, says that "they are instructed in letters and arms in the same manner as the
children of the sultan." [1] Ottaviano Bon, who held the
post of Venetian *bailo*, the most distinguished post
of the diplomatic corps at Constantinople, wrote in
1608:

The course that is pursued with the pages is not that of a
barbaric people, but rather that of a people of singular virtue
and self-discipline. From the time that they first enter the
school of the Grand Seraglio they are exceedingly well-
directed. Day by day they are continuously instructed in
good and comely behavior, in the discipline of the senses, in
military prowess, and in a knowledge of the Moslem faith;
in a word, in all the virtues of mind and body. [2]

Michel Baudier, official historiographer of France, a
laborious and estimable scholar, whose *Histoire généralle
du Serrail* first appeared in 1624, says of the value of
the palace educational system:

It is not astonishing that the Turkish nation prospers, since the Turks know so well how to choose the *élite* from great numbers of youths and how to give them the instruction and the discipline which makes them honest men, thus adjusting to the gifts of nature the perfections of art. . . . The order and the method with which these youths are trained, show certainly that the Turks have retained nothing of barbarism except the name.[3]

The French humanist, Blaise de Vigenère, who in 1660 translated Chalcocondyles' *Histoire de la décadence de l'empire Grec, et établissement des Turcs*, appending to this translation certain researches of his own on the contemporary condition of the Ottoman Empire, observed with exceptional acumen for his age: "It should be understood, first of all, that the whole establishment of the sultan's court, the foundation of his empire, and the strength of his army, depend upon a permanent seminary of young boys." [4] Sir Paul Rycaut, "Late Secretary to his Excellency the Earl of Winchelsea (Embassador Extraordinary for his Majesty Charles the Second) and now British Consul at Smyrna," author of *The Present State of the Ottoman Empire*, and one of the earliest of Europeans to make a special study of the Turkish state and the Moslem faith, writing in 1668, adjudged the palace training to be, "if well considered and weighed, one of the most Politick Constitutions in the World, and none of the meanest supports of the *Ottoman* Empire." [5]

The proof, or measure, of the importance of the Palace School is seen in the fact that, during the two centuries which succeeded its organization by Muhammad II, the majority of the officials of the court and government, the officers as well as the rank and file of the regular cavalry or cavalry of the Sublime Porte (*Sipahis*), the superior officers of the navy, and, for a time, the chiefs of the Janizary corps, were the products of its training.[6] Of the sixty grand viziers whose careers the Turkish historian Tayyar Zadeh Ata Bey has traced, forty-eight were trained in the Palace School, or Inner Service, of the Grand Seraglio, as compared with the remaining twelve, who rose to the post from the outer service of the palace. Among the more famous of those trained in the school may be mentioned: Khervat (Croat) Mahmud Pasha, first grand vizir of Muhammad II after the conquest of Constantinople and seventh grand vizir of the dynasty; four grand viziers of Suleiman the Magnificent, Lutfi Pasha, Ibrahim Pasha, Rustem Pasha, and Soqullu Muhammad Pasha; Djighala-zadeh Sinan Pasha (better known to Europeans as Cicala Pasha), hero of the famous cavalry charge at the battle of Cerestes and thereby grand vizir; Kiuprulu Muhammad Pasha, the founder of the family of grand viziers of that name; Damad Ibrahim Pasha; and Qibrisli (Cyprian) Mehmed Emin Pasha, one of the last graduates of the Palace School before it ceased to be a school of state, one of the first Turks to study in Europe, and one of the most active influences in the introduction of civil and military reforms into Turkey. In the list of other officials educated in the Palace School, Ata includes twenty-three lords of the admiralty, as compared with eleven who were promoted to that position from the outer service of the Grand Seraglio; twenty-three sword-bearers; an innumerable host of minor officials; a number of distinguished writers and artists; and three *sheykhs-ul-Islam* — in spite of the fact that the training of the Palace School did not lead to this last line of service.[7]

So perfectly did the Palace School mold aliens of widely divergent race and creed to the Turkish type, and so thoroughgoing was the process of assimilation, that there are on record few instances of rebels or renegades among officials educated within its walls. When compared with the chronic disaffection and turbulence of the Janizaries (*Yenicheri*), who received a type of barrack education vastly inferior to that of the Palace School, the loyalty of the pages is particularly striking. Not only did the pages prove able and zealous officials, but in great crises they frequently gave proof of extraordinary personal loyalty to the dynasty. In 1703, at the time of the assassination of the Sheykh-ul-Islam Feyzullah Efendi, which resulted in an insurrection of the Janizaries and the flight of the grand vizir and other members of the Divan, it was the pages of the Grand Seraglio who saved the life of Mustafa II by spiriting him away to the palace in Adrianople. And again upon the deposition and death of Selim III, it was a page in the Grand Seraglio, the father of the historian Ata, Tayyar Efendi, who at great risk to himself saved the life of the heir-apparent, the only remaining scion of the dynasty,[8] afterwards Mahmud II.

In view of the far-reaching influence of the Palace School, the question naturally arises why modern historians have failed to perceive its significance. Mouradja d'Ohsson and von Hammer-Purgstall, both of whom have written monumental histories of the Ottoman Empire, describe the page system, but have failed to recognize its full political significance and have missed entirely its educational character. Von Hammer even blunders to the extent of classifying the pages as servants (*hof bedienten*),[9] whereas by Turks they are always referred to as either *talebeh* [10] (students) or *oghlanlar* (pages). The great von Ranke grasped the slave and page systems, but gives no indication of having apprehended the educational system beyond the single statement that, to the inexorable discipline to which the Janizaries were submitted, the palace education "added literary and somewhat knightly tasks." [11] The Rumanian historian, Professor N. Jorga, who has written the best recent history of the Ottoman Empire, makes only incidental mention of the school. Professor Albert Howe Lybyer, in his scholarly treatise, *The Government of the Ottoman Empire in the Reign of Suleiman the Magnificent*, published in 1913, was the first to rediscover the educational character of the Palace School and its great importance in the Turkish polity. The present monograph seeks to supply fuller knowledge of the founding of the school, of its organization and personnel, of its life, and of the curriculum, which is, perhaps, its most distinctive feature.

CHAPTER I

THE GENESIS OF THE PALACE SCHOOL

IN THE fifteenth century a military school of state was a bold and highly original conception, for which no one single prototype or model seems to have existed. In spite of the efficiency of the Arab political system, no evidence has been discovered of any systematic training for government service. Nor, indeed, has it been possible to find in earlier Islam formal institutions for higher education of any sort with the exception of the early mosque schools; the academies for translation of Hellenic literature into Arabic, the *dar ul-hikma* (houses of wisdom), which flourished from 750 to 900 A.D. and became centers of propaganda for the heretical Shiites; and the *medresehs*,[1] theological seminaries established by the Sunni, the orthodox sect of Islam, during the first half of the eleventh century A.D., to train the Ulema, the body of Moslem jurists, and at the same time to counteract the Shiah and Fatimid influences.

Because of the lack of continuity and the consequent absence of historical data, it has not been possible to determine if the University of Constantinople[2] during the early period of its existence provided training for the bureaucracy which was such a distinguishing feature of the Byzantine Empire in the Middle Ages. At the time of its revival by Constantine Porphyrogenitus (912–959 A.D.), the university emerges for the first time

unmistakably as a "higher school of administration."
Revived again by Constantine Monomachus in 1045 as
a part of the general renaissance of the eleventh century,
it includes certain resemblances to the Palace School of
Muhammad the Conqueror, which may, or may not,
indicate Byzantine influence upon the Palace School.
The power having passed from the aristocratic and military castes to the crown, it becomes evident that the
chief purpose of Constantine Monomachus in reviving
the university was the training of a new bureaucracy
built, like that of Muhammad, upon the essentially
democratic basis of a merit system, and not, as heretofore, upon the foundation of a senatorial nobility.
Like the Palace School, the university was state-
supported and was entirely secular in character, the
outstanding example of the cleavage between ecclesiastical and lay education which had existed from earliest
times in the eastern Roman Empire. Although there is
no suggestion in the curriculum of the university of the
extraordinary combination of the intellectual, physical,
and vocational training which was such a conspicuous
characteristic of the Palace School, there was in both
institutions, confined strictly within the orbits of the
two widely differing civilizations, marked emphasis
upon the law, as was natural in any school of government, and at times, perhaps, even greater emphasis upon
the humanities, which as Rambaud remarked, "in the
Greek Empire seemed indispensable and even sufficient
for statesmen." Minor resemblances were the gratui-
tous instruction, including incidental expenses, of the
students, and the very high rank accorded the more
notable professors. Another instrument for bureaucratic

training, less formal than the university, was the cloisters, from which students are said to have passed directly into the administrative and military services, but concerning which little is known. The highly specialized Byzantine schools under the supervision of scholars for notaries, archivists, secretaries, *et cetera*, which are believed to have existed within the administration itself afford no points of comparison with the Palace School of the sultans, sequestered as it was within the forbidden precincts of the Grand Seraglio.

The nearest approach to an analogy or prototype for the Palace School of the Turkish sultans is to be found in a development of the *medreseh*, when the Seljuk Turks, an older branch of the Turkish stock than the Ottomans, made a departure from the typical seminary by attaching to certain *medresehs* additional colleges, or sections, for instruction in secular subjects, the commonest of these being "science and philosophy as they were taught among the Greeks," and "the art and science of government." In the years 1065–1067 A.D., Nizam ul-Mulk, grand vizir of the Seljuk sultans Alp Arslan and Malik Shah, and ruler of the Seljukian Empire for more than twenty years in all but name, founded in Baghdad the celebrated Nizamiyah *Medreseh*, which appears to have included two sections: one a seminary for the study of the *Shafiite* school of canon law and for the propagation of the *Ashari* system of scholastic theology; [3] and a second for the instruction of those intended "*for places in the public administration.*" Nizam ul-Mulk, Persian in origin and boyhood friend of Omar Khayyam, was one of the greatest patrons of higher learning and one of the most constructive statesmen ever produced in Islam. In the words of Professor Philip Hitti, "Nizam's glory is his establishment of the first well-organized academies for higher learning in Islam."

Nizam's chief motive in founding the Nizamiyah, "whose beauty," to quote from the words of the famous traveler, Ibn Batuta (1325–1354), "has given birth to proverbs," is said to have been a desire to win, by the establishment of pious foundations, the favor of the powerful Ulema, who, besides filling all religious and legal offices of the Empire, controlled all matters connected with law and every phase of learning. Reason enough for the establishment of a school of state may perhaps be found in Nizam ul-Mulk's own long political career and in his interest in statesmanship as it is revealed in his one book, the *Siasset Nameh*, a manual for rulers similar to *The Prince* of Machiavelli. But a special reason suggests itself in the most difficult of the problems which Nizam ul-Mulk, as a practical statesman, faced: the necessity of providing some kind of training and organization, beyond that of a tribal army, for the large number of Turcomans that had been attracted into the Empire by reason of the Seljukian successes. In the *Siasset Nameh*, Nizam ul-Mulk urges specifically the continued employment of these bands in the sultan's service and the provision of some kind of training for them:

The Turcomans, in spite of having caused serious difficulties and of being considerable in number, are nevertheless entitled to the goodwill of the present dynasty because they rendered numerous services at the time of its establishment, because they have endured much for it, and because they are con-

nected with it by ties of kinship. It is therefore necessary to
inscribe the names of a thousand of their children upon the
registers and to assign to them, as to the *ghoulams* [slaves of
the Court] a special residence. As they must remain con-
tinually attached to the service, they will learn the handling
of arms and the service of the Court.[4]

In case of need, Nizam continues, from five to ten
thousand of these slaves can be assembled who will
render service in the same manner as the *ghoulams*.
This custom of employing large numbers of Turkish
slaves as the personal guard of the sovereign was begun
by the Abbasid caliphs [5] and continued by the Persian
Samanids and later in the eastern Moslem states. In
the extremely intricate bureaucracy of the Samanids
(874–999 A.D.) these slaves, after serving a long and
highly systematized apprenticeship, became eligible
for the highest offices in the two main categories of
the Samanid political organization, the palace and the
chancery; and also, after the age of thirty-five, for the
highest military offices, especially the provincial governorships. "Representative of the old Persian culture"
and bureaucracy, Nizam ul-Mulk almost certainly was
familiar with the training provided by the Samanids
for their Turkish slaves,[6] and very possibly developed
his *madrasah politique* from this pattern.

In confirmation of the political character of the Nizamiyah type of *medreseh*, which he calls the *madrasah
politique*, the celebrated Swiss Arabist and epigraphist,
Max von Berchem (1863–1921), has assembled the
following evidence:

I believe that the special contribution of Nizam ul-Mulk
is to have founded schools of state, veritable seminaries, *sorte*

de pépinières officielles pour toutes les charges publiques. This character is confirmed by a number of distinguishing characteristics. The professors were chosen by the founders themselves, who determined all the details of organization. It was no longer the free, or private *madrasah,* that the professor directed according to his own caprice, which became more and more rare after the eleventh century, although the mosque schools continued to flourish side by side with the *madrasah.* In order to teach in a *madrasah* it was necessary to have an official diploma,[7] while the mosque schools remained freer in this respect. Further, the founder paid and lodged the professors, often the pupils themselves, thus reserving the right to direct them as he chose. Another trait which revealed the *madrasah* as the personal project of the sultans was that they were accustomed to attach their mausoleums to *madrasahs;* as, for example, the sultans of Cairo, nearly all of whom are interred in *madrasahs,* and rarely in mosques, properly speaking. In reexamining these and other characteristic details in the light of the political and religious revolution which reached its height at the epoch of Nizam, the historic role of the *madrasah* appears in its true light.[8]

In contradicting the contention of Arab historians that the Nizamiyah was the first *medreseh* in point of time, MacGuckin de Slane, translator and editor of the great *Biographical Dictionary* by Ibn Khallikan, incidentally bears further witness to the civil and secular character of the Nizamiyah:

It may be concluded that Nizâm al-Mulk founded neither the first *madrasa* nor the first academy, and that the institution called after him the *Nizâmiya* was merely one of the earliest *civil* establishments for the propagation of learning; the talent of its professors shed, it is true, a brilliant lustre upon its reputation, but the mosques continued nevertheless to be the only regular academies acknowledged by the law.[9]

The wide fame of the Nizamiyah was not due to priority in date,[10] as has already been said, nor were its land-endowed scholarships an innovation, as has been frequently asserted. Rather, its renown is to be attributed to the generous and energetic support of its founder; to the institution of a boarding department, which later became the prevailing type of all *medresehs*; and to the brilliance of its teachers, among whom the best known was al-Ghazzali, "unquestionably the greatest theologian in Islam and one of its noblest and most original thinkers," who "fixed the ultimate form of the *Ashariyah* and established its dicta as the final form for Sunnite orthodoxy."

How far-reaching were the effects of the founding of the Nizamiyah may be seen quite clearly in a second excerpt from von Berchem:

Later Nizam ul-Mulk founded other *madrasahs* at Basra, Isfahan, Balkh, Herat, Mosul, and elsewhere. His successors imitated his example and the *madrasah* spread throughout the length and breadth of the Seljuk Empire. That which he did for Persia and Chaldea, the great vassals of the Seljuks, the Atabeys of Mosul and Damascus, Nur ad-Din and Saladin, who also became the champions of the Sunnite reaction, did for Mesopotamia, Syria and Egypt. . . . The *madrasah* spread everywhere from Samarcand to the Sudan.[11]

From the ninth to the twelfth century the great schools of Iraq continued to be the chief centers of learning throughout the Moslem world. Their influence extended even to Moslem Spain, where it is said to have led to the founding of higher institutions of learning and to the introduction of scholastic theology. The movement is even believed by some authorities to have influenced the founding of European universities some two hundred years later.

In the early period of the *medreseh* of the seminary type, the principal studies were the Koran and old poetry, which together formed, again to quote Professor Hitti, the humanities of Islam, "precisely as the classics did later in the European universities." As systems of law and theology developed, these were added. Gradually the "science of Tradition" was evolved to a point where it became the basis of the curriculum. Frequently a *medreseh* became famous for some one specialty, as did the Nizamiyah in philology, which was ranked next to the Koran and Traditions in importance. Philosophy proper was banned. A certificate, or licence, from a *medreseh* conferred the rank of Doctor of Law and Tradition and led directly to a career as preacher (*khatib*), leader of daily prayers (*imam*), judge (*qadi*), professor (*muderris*), and head of the Ulema (*mufti*, or *sheikh ul-Islam*). In a consideration of the course of study in the government section of the Nizamiyah, MacGuckin de Slane has deduced from the functions of the provincial governors the following conclusions as to the necessary qualifications for their secretaries (*katibs*):

It is much more difficult to mark out the line of study followed by those who were destined to fill places in the public administration. The *kâtib* should be not only, as his name implies, a good penman, but also a master of the beauties of the Arabic language, well acquainted with grammar and the writings of the poets, a skilful accountant and gifted with a capacity for business. Some *kâtibs* were employed to draw up state papers; others, to keep the public accounts and registers, or to receive the tithes and the revenues of the state;

every governor of a province had his *kâtib* [as Nizam ul-Mulk himself was *katib* to the governor of Balkh] whose duty was to keep the correspondence, and to receive the taxes of the district, the rents of the government farms, etc. Out of this money a fixed sum was yearly remitted to the sovereign, the governor reserving the rest for his own use and the payment of the troops, and persons entitled to salaries, such as the *kâdis*, the juriconsults, the *imams* of the great mosques, the clerks in the public offices, etc. Part of it was absorbed also by works of public utility, and in defraying the expenses of his court. He was obliged besides to maintain the post-horse establishment, but the postmaster, who acted as a spy over the governor, was nominated by the sovereign.[12]

The suggestion by MacGuckin de Slane that the course of study of the Nizamiyah combined training in government with instruction in the liberal arts is further borne out by the curriculum of the universities of Moslem Spain, which, as has already been said, are thought to have developed as the result of the influence of the Nizamiyah. It is supported also by the type of training for slave officials and princes of the royal line provided by some of the successors of the Seljuk dynasty, the later Turkish rulers of Central Asia and Moslem rulers of India, who could scarcely have escaped so widespread an influence as that of the Nizamiyah. The preparation for government service in the Spanish universities included the Koran, "as the root and inspiration of all the sciences," Arabic literature, biographical and genealogical histories, mathematics (usually in connection with other studies), and "a little music, which was not held in very high esteem." The teaching of law was especially emphasized, including instruction in notarial and judicial procedure and "a definite and profound analysis of contracts and inheritance." Jurisprudence was the most popular of all studies. Out of the waning influence of the traditions, it is said, came the development of *là politica*, the art of government, from which proceeded "what is, perhaps, the most important book written in Moslem Spain, the *Lampara de Principes* of Abubequer el Tortuxi." In the teaching of Arabic literature, by which was meant history, short anecdote, poetry, and rhymed prose, "the ability to write rhymed prose in particular marked a man as cultured and intellectual; proficiency in these subjects led directly to positions as court secretaries, ministers, judges and governors." [13] In the courts at Ghazni, Agra, and Delhi, the same combination of government and liberal arts is also found. In what is today Afghanistan, Muhammad of Ghor (1149–1161 A.D.), successor to the Ghazni dynasty and "the first real conqueror of India," "took pleasure in educating the Turkey slaves whom he afterwards adopted, combining a literary education with a training in the difficult art of practical government." Sultan Firuz (1351–1388 A.D.) of the Tughlaq dynasty was "trained in his youth in the art of government by his uncle Ghiyassudin Tughlaq. . . . His literary education was equally satisfactory." Sultan Sikander (1488–1518 A.D.) of the Lodi dynasty "insisted that all of his officers should be educated. This gave a new character to the profession of arms, in which military virtues had to be combined with the literary qualifications." Akbar the Great (1556–1605 A.D.), whose uncommon thirst for knowledge and catholicity of literary taste are strongly reminiscent of Muhammad the Conqueror, included government and history in his new curriculum.[14]

The Nizamiyah was thoroughly renovated in 504 A.H.

(1110/11 A.D.). The traveler Ibn Jubair, who visited Baghdad in 1185, describes it as the most splendid of the thirty-odd colleges which then adorned the fashionable quarter of East Baghdad. It was still in good condition when Ibn Batuta visited the city in 1327 and it survived the conquest by Timur in 1393, but two years later it was merged with its rival, the Mustansiriyeh *Medreseh*, which also stood in the great market street of the same quarter and which, founded in 1234 by the Caliph al-Mustansir to eclipse the Nizamiyah, is said to have "surpassed everything hitherto known in Islam." [15] The buildings of the *Nizamiyah* had completely disappeared when the explorer Carsten Niebuhr (1733–1815) visited Baghdad. It seems reasonable to believe that Muhammad the Conqueror, with his extraordinary command of languages, with his prodigious love of learning of every sort, his passion for surrounding himself with distinguished men of letters drawn from east and west alike, and his very special interest in education, would have had knowledge of so famous a Turkish school as the Nizamiyah, which had lost its separate identity little more than half a century before the founding of his Palace School. He may well have taken from it the idea of making his school a school of government and the liberal arts, as well as a school of war.

The material for his student body Muhammad certainly found at hand ready-made in two older institutions: the slave system of government and the system of royal pages. The slave system of government has been commonly supposed to be oriental, and its most familiar example is that of the Mamluk dynasty of

Egypt. A recent theory suggests that the Byzantines also used this form of government in spirit, if not in actual fact, and that there is a direct connection in this particular between the Ottoman and Byzantine empires.[16] However that may be, from earliest times it had been a characteristic tendency of the Turks, as also of the Mongols, to recruit by a system of adoption the official class of their politico-military organization, their warrior-statesmen, from alien sources. After their arrival in Asia Minor, when their domain was but a petty fief of the Seljuk sultans, their small warrior band maintained and expanded its authority, not solely by means of military superiority but also by means of absorption into their governing class of prisoners-of-war [17] drawn from the more advanced races whom they conquered. As their power prevailed, the Turks attracted to themselves adventurers and renegades of every description and with equal ease assimilated them into their army and official class. All became, in theory at least, slaves (*qul*) of the sultan. Beginning with the Law of Draft of Murad I (1360–1389), by far the largest number of recruits from any one single source were drawn from the tribute children levied upon the subject races of the Balkans. So it came about that, by the time of Muhammad II, the official class was composed largely of slaves who were, in origin, of alien blood and alien creed. Synchronously with this development of a slave system of government went a corresponding expansion in the number of royal pages, an institution which dates back to the time when Brusa was the Turkish capital. To both of these institutions, some system of education was a natural corollary.

The reign of Murad II, father of Muhammad II, is esteemed to have been

of extraordinary importance for the future political and cultural history of the Ottoman Empire. . . . The mystical tradition was strong in his surroundings, as is proved by the great influence of a man like the Shaikh Amir Bukhari; other shaikhs came to his court from Persia and Mesopotamia. This determined also the direction which the Ottoman classical literature was to take in following centuries. Murad II was the first Ottoman prince whose court became a brilliant centre of poets, literary men, and Muhammadan scholars. But also to non-Moslem envoys and visitors Murad's court seemed a centre of culture.[18]

It would seem that formal instruction of the royal pages began with the Princes' School of Murad II, since no evidence has been found that the royal pages received any instruction outside the practice of arms before his reign. In his remarkable memoirs, Johann Schiltberger, a German who was taken prisoner at the battle of Nicopolis and who served as a page for six years in the royal palaces of Brusa and Adrianople during the reign of Bayazid I (1389–1402), says no more of his training or duties than that "I was obliged to run on my feet with the others whenever he (the Sultan) went, it being the custom that the Turkish lords have people to run before them."[19] In the reign of Murad II, however, a number of the royal pages and several Greek princes who were retained as hostages at the Turkish court were educated with the heir-apparent in the royal palace at Adrianople.[20] As royal preceptors (*hunkiar hojasilar*) Murad employed a series of scholars and legists who were among the most distinguished and enlightened men in the empire. Among them may be noted especially the Mullah Kurani, the Mullah Sirek (*sic*), the savants Khojazadeh and Khatibzadeh, the mathematician Mirem Chelebi, and the poet Ahmed Pasha,[21] in turn judge of the army (*qadiasker*) and vizir after the accession of his royal pupil. It is interesting that the most celebrated poem of this famous poet, with whom the history of Ottoman poetry is said to have begun, should have been a description of the Grand Seraglio, and also that he should have suffered banishment because of a poem sympathizing with a recalcitrant page of the Palace School. It seems probable that this Princes' School in Adrianople was the forerunner of the great school of state in the royal palace in Constantinople.

Chief among the pages educated with Prince Muhammad was Khervat (Croat) Mahmud Pasha, a tribute child purchased by Mehemet Agha, one of the officers of Murad's court, and presented by him to the sultan. Admitted into the Adrianople palace in the capacity of a page, the boy was later attached to the service of the Treasury. Of the same age as the young Prince Muhammad and noticeably clever, Mahmud was transferred to him and became his boyhood familiar, the rival companion of his studies, and, as has already been said, his first grand vizir after the conquest of Constantinople. As a result of a quarrel with Prince Mustafa, son of Muhammad, and a rumor that the subsequent death of the prince was due to poison, Mahmud Pasha was exiled and later put to death by order of the sultan — a fate which reminds one of the tragic dénouement of the friendship between Suleiman and his favorite, the celebrated Grand Vizir Ibrahim Pasha. By reason of his scholarly attainments Mahmud Pasha has been sometimes called "the first graduate of the Palace School" and "the first Grand Vizir worthy of the name." [22] Still another page educated with Muhammad was the Albanian, George Castriota, better known to Europeans as Scanderbey from his Turkish name (Iskender Bey), one of the four sons of the Prince of Epirus held as hostages at the imperial court. His position there and the training which he received are described as follows:

Amorathe [Murad II] truely semed to be exceding glad when Scanderbeg (being a childe but of eyghte yeres of age) was broughte to his presence, and seinge him beautifull & to have a majeste in his countenance, he jugged in hymselfe that yf he shoulde lyve longe, he wolde prove a worthye man, wherefore he determyned never to suffer him to retorne home againe, but to kepe him in his courte, to the end that when he was comme to the state of a man he shoulde serve him, and therfore appointed him worthy masters to instruct him, & to be carefull for him and to se him broughte up in lerning, and civilitie he allowed both for his table and apparell even as yf he had ben his onne sonne. After this when Scanderbeg was somethinge growen he delyghted to ryde, and to ronne and also with his companions to use the launce and sworde, and he dyd excede them all bothe on horsebacke, and on fote.[23]

He was made *sanjak bey* at nineteen years of age and put in command of five thousand horse. Having deserted from the sultan's army and seized Croia, the chief city of Epirus, for twenty years he led revolt after revolt against the Turks, and yet — perhaps on account of his youthful association with Sultan Muhammad — was never so thoroughly punished as he would otherwise most certainly have been.

The earliest source of information concerning the

Palace School that has been found is the *Historia turchesca* of Gio(vanni) Maria Angiolello. Angiolello was a scion of a patrician family of Vicenza who was taken captive at the siege of Negropont in 1470 and who spent many years as a page in the service of the Grand Seraglio. In his opinion — and he seems to have been extraordinarily judicial and restrained for a captive of his age — Prince Muhammad had "a splendid mind and many gifts." As the result of these natural capacities and tastes, in particular of his great love of learning, which had been deepened and directed by his father's wise provision for his education, Muhammad's intellectual attainments far surpassed those of any other scion of the Ottoman dynasty. For a Turk of the fifteenth century, he possessed extraordinary linguistic ability; he had a thorough knowledge of literary Turkish, as may be seen in his mastery of the formal epistolary prose style of the period; he also knew well Arabic, Persian, and Greek, and is said to have been able to speak "a corrupt Italian." Even before his accession at the age of twenty-one he kept himself informed of the intellectual and artistic movements throughout the Moslem world by correspondence and very friendly relations with various rulers: with the grandson of Timur, Baysunghur, and his son, Abd al-Latif; with Jihan Shah, a prince of the dynasty of the Black Sheep; with the rulers of Shirvan and Herat, and with numerous others. Himself a poet, Muhammad enjoyed the society of poets, especially Persian poets; he gathered them in numbers about him, from Moslem lands of the East, and treated them with great generosity, granting pensions to thirty Turkish poets, in addition to annual pensions of one thousand ducats each to Khoja Jami, the foremost writer of the age in India, and to the Mullah Jami, the last great poet of Persia. To the latter, Muhammad also sent a special purse of five thousand ducats for the pilgrimage to Mecca, and with it an invitation to reside at his court.[24] Unfortunately for such generosity, Mullah Jami, having set out from Khorasan before receiving the gift, arrived first at the court of Shah Uzun-Hasan, and was beguiled by this monarch into remaining there. Muhammad also delighted generally in philosophy, both oriental and Greek. To Ali Qushji (Ali the Fowler), an illustrious philosopher from Samarcand, Muhammad paid one thousand *aqchas* * for each stage of the long journey to his court. He continued to read history throughout his life, especially the lives of his favorite heroes, Alexander the Great and the Caesars.

His signal victories and successes throughout the course of his life afforded ample proof of the profound knowledge which he had acquired by the reading of every sort of good books; especially histories in which he took such great pleasure that he caused nearly all histories to be translated into his language; and he honored so much those who excelled in historical knowledge, as also in the other arts and sciences, that he welcomed warmly all these at his court and incited them to create beautiful things by means of the generous rewards which he gave them.

Barthélémy d'Herbelot, writing in 1697, adds that Muhammad was "not ignorant even of Greek and Latin history and that several of our books, of which we find yet some versions in the Turkish language, are dedicated

* Fifty *aqchas* had the value of one Venetian gold ducat.

to him." [25] Above all else he was a student of the history
and the science of war, the fruit of which study is seen
in his mastery of strategy and in his thorough knowledge of everything connected with munitions and the
commissariat. In sports he excelled in the use of the
masse d'armes, in horsemanship, and in archery.[26] In
conformity with the old Turkish tradition that everyone,
even royalty, should be trained in some one trade or
craft that might prove a resource in event of misfortune,
Muhammad became a gardener, attaining such skill in
this occupation and deriving such pleasure from it that
he spent much of his leisure, in the intervals between
campaigns, working in the gardens of the Grand Seraglio
and other royal palaces.

The education of Muhammad and the high value
which he set upon education and upon intellectual attainments of every kind, are important not only for
their far-reaching effect upon his own character and per-
sonality — it has been remarked that the variations
and contradictions of his conduct at times are inex-
plicable unless they be regarded as the result of a conflict
between his natural characteristics and those which
were acquired through training and education — but
also for their far-reaching effect upon Turkish state
institutions. It is certainly more than a coincidence
that there was no important phase of his own tastes or
training which was not later reproduced in his Palace
School. A further effect may be seen in his generous
patronage of individual students, scholars, and men of
letters, and in the high rank which he accorded them in
his reorganization of the educational system of the
medresehs. In this same connection an estimate by the

Turkish historian Saad ad-Din of Muhammad's generous services in behalf of education and scholarship, and of his own natural gifts and achievements in the pursuit of knowledge, has especial interest:

He was generally regretted by all his subjects, particularly by those who had distinguished themselves in letters and in science during his reign, because of the marks of esteem and consideration they had received from him in the shape of liberalities. . . .

The protection he extended to men of letters has resulted in the production of innumerable works of value, the majority of which are dedicated to him. In the manner of his ancestors he was accustomed to give alms each Friday, on so generous a scale that it would be too great an undertaking to give a detailed list of the gratuities which he bestowed upon men of letters, *sheikhs* or other people devoted to the cult of God, and the descendants of the Prophet.

Nothing greater or more magnificent could be imagined than the mosque which he caused to be built in the city of Stambul . . . and the eight colleges destined to teach the sciences which surround it, each college having eight apartments of several rooms each for the purpose of housing the students. There is also a soup kitchen [*imaret*] where morning and evening abundant meats are cooked for the poor of both sexes, as also for the students who eat in a large refectory built for that purpose. In this same place may be seen a hostel for foreign travellers, equipped with a separate kitchen, stables both for their mounts and their beasts of burden, and a large storehouse where is provided barley and straw with which to feed them. There is also an infirmary for the poor with a separate bath and everything else necessary to take care of them. There is even a school to teach the children how to read. The funds with which these foundations are endowed, which are under the direction of the *qadi* of Stambul, are so ample that there remains a sufficient sum for pensions for the doctors of law [*mullahs*], the *sheikhs*, the de-

scendants of the Prophet, men of letters, and all other holders
of great offices who have acquitted themselves with credit.

In the vicinity of Stambul Muhammad also caused to be
built a beautiful domed mausoleum above the grave of Abu
Eyyub [27] of Medina, friend and standard-bearer of the
Prophet, and by the side of the mausoleum an equally beautiful mosque with two minarets. He installed there a teacher
who received fifty *aqchas* a day for giving instruction in the
Traditions. Connected with this mosque there are also apartments for students and a soup kitchen in the same quarter
where they receive their food, as do also the poor of the same
district. . . . He also collected several thousand manuscripts, in most instances autograph copies of the rarest and
most valuable commentaries and exigeses on Islamic law and
religion, and caused them to be distributed in each of the
mosques which he had built for the use and convenience of
the teachers residing in these mosques. In short, he forgot
none of the good works he could do in this world. . . .

In conclusion, so great was his genius and so deeply had he
gone into the sciences that the greatest scholars of his day were
filled with wonder and praise. By means of the great and
unusual knowledge which he acquired he reigned with a wisdom and prudence that commanded universal admiration.[28]

In the year of the conquest of Constantinople, when
Muhammad was only twenty-four years of age, it is
recorded by Johann Loewenklau that "in addition to
the usual royal beneficences to paupers and widows he
caused gifts to be distributed to students and doctors
of law, and that upon the latter he also conferred grants
of land which yielded monthly incomes."[29] He gave the
royal preceptors unprecedentedly high rank. Throughout his reign they were attached as much to his own
person as to that of the young heir-apparent, Prince
Bayazid. It was Muhammad who first elevated the
post of royal preceptor to a government appointment

by attaching it to the order of the Ulema and by plac-
ing it in the first five classes of that carefully graded
hierarchy. In the court ceremonial at the two *Bayrams*
the royal preceptor took precedence over the vizirs,
the two judges of the army, and the treasurers, and on
other public occasions occupied what was the second
position of honor, to the right of the sultan, the head of
the Ulema (the *Mufti*, later *Sheikh ul-Islam*), occupying the first position of honor to the left.[30] With the aid
of the grand vizir, Croat Mahmud Pasha, he fixed the
hierarchical order of the Ulema and organized the curriculum of the *medreseh* into ten branches: grammar,
syntax, science of tropes, science of style, rhetoric, logic,
metaphysics, geometry, astronomy, and astrology.
Pressure was put even upon officials already long in the
service of the state — vizirs, legists, and other great
pashas — who, in the hope of gaining the royal favor,
began to apply themselves assiduously to the study of
literature and the sciences. The movement spread, and
learning and literature became the fashion of the reign.[31]
Later, by means of generous gifts, pensions, and similar
inducements, Muhammad drew from many directions
men of distinction who formed a veritable Academy of
Letters at his court.[32] Turkish writers agree in speaking
of the reign as a kind of golden age; at no time and
among no people, says Latifeh, was learning more
highly esteemed.[33]

In his passion for learning Muhammad even organized a system of education for the women of his harem.
Of slave origin, like the pages, it is reported on excellent contemporary authority that "these women are
taught to speak and read Turkish, they are instructed

in Moslem law, and they also learn to sew, embroider, play the harp, sing, and all other accomplishments according as they have the inclination to learn." The extent to which they profited from such opportunity may be judged somewhat by the attainments of Herzisdad (Hurmazdad?) Sultan, daughter of Prince Mustafa and grand-daughter of the Conqueror. Upon the arrival of her father's funeral cortège in Brusa, the burial place of the early sultans, she delivered an oration

which lasted more than an hour, in which she praised his virtues and mentioned by name some of the people who had been brought up with him, saying that, had he survived, the world would have known much better his good will towards his followers; and that death was the common lot of all. She said many other things which made her hearers all to weep, even Herzisdad herself being obliged to stop and weep at suitable moments, which she did with very decorous movements and gestures, showing at the same time a great audacity. For all that she said and did she was much praised, as much for her wisdom as for her erudition in Arabic literature and expert knowledge on every subject pertaining to a woman of her condition. So that her fame spread as far as Constantinople, and even in other countries people talked of the qualities and virtues of this young woman.[34]

It is probable that the immediate occasion of the founding of the Palace School by Muhammad was an urgent need, especially following the conquest of Constantinople, for both civil and military officials in a rapidly expanding empire, and possibly, also, a dissatisfaction with the type of official which had previously been produced by the apprentice method or in the entirely practical experience of office-holding or of war.

His motive has been interpreted by the Turkish historian Tayyar Zadeh Ata Bey as follows:

Impressed by the great loyalty of the pages and convinced that it would be impossible to find more faithful servants and friends to help him preserve his throne against the attacks of outside enemies and of the Janizaries, the sultan conceived the idea of rearing and educating in adequate numbers in a general school [mekteb-i umumi] in his royal palace the type of valiant soldier and scholarly official which was so badly needed for all the functions of the empire.[35]

Under Muhammad's enlightened direction the Palace School expanded and took on the definite character of a school of government, and so perfect an instrument did it prove for the purpose for which it was designed that its perpetuation and development became one of the most conscious policies and most powerful traditions of his successors. Primarily and essentially secular in its purpose — of which no better proof exists than the fact that the student scholarships and the pay of the entire personnel were disbursed from the Bureau of Infantry — the Palace School of the Turkish sultans was a greater departure from the theological or *medreseh* type of education than the medieval university was from the monastic and cathedral schools.

Certainly no period in Turkish history was more favorable for the development of a great school of state than the time of Muhammad's accession, and no sultan could have been more fitted than Muhammad to set the direction of its growth and to be its presiding genius. Besides the "two permanent teachers" resident in the Grand Seraglio of whom Angiolello speaks, in an account of the school to be quoted later, the nucleus of the faculty must almost certainly have been the dozen or more royal preceptors drawn from among the various ranks of the Ulema attached to the *medresehs* in the city, and from among the numerous savants whom Muhammad had gathered about himself from every point of the compass, veritably converting his palace, as Ata says, into a school (*mekteb*). Usually these preceptors were doctors of law (*mullahs*) and among the most distinguished members of the Ulema, corresponding to the bishops of the palace school of Charlemagne. But it is especially noteworthy that, within the fraternity of learning and letters resident at Muhammad's court, there were to be found Christians as well as Moslems, among whom were a number of Greeks. A recent Turkish biographer of Muhammad, Namiq Kemal Bey, says that, following the conquest of Constantinople, Muhammad made a great effort to stop the flight to Italy of Greek scholars, writers, teachers, philosophers, and men of letters in general, and to retain as many as possible in the capital, and that he employed Greek scribes for the purpose of diplomatic correspondence with Venice, Genoa, and Rhodes, and also as official chroniclers, a custom that was continued until the reign of Selim II.[36]

Among the more notable Greeks who were attached to the court of Muhammad was the historian Critoboulos, who entered the Turkish service about the time of the conquest of Constantinople. He was later governor of Imbros until it was occupied by the Venetians in 1466, after which it is probable that he went to Constantinople. He wrote a life of Muhammad II, which for its accuracy and intimate acquaintance with the affairs of the court is reckoned one of the most valuable of the period. A Greek whose work is less known than that of Critoboulos, but who probably exerted more influence upon the sultan and doubtless, in an indirect way, upon the school, was the philosopher George Amyrutzes, who accompanied the Emperor David Paleologus to Constantinople after the fall of Trebizond, shortly thereafter "turning Turk with all his children, and receiving great employment in the Seraglio." A high authority on the systems of the Peripatetics and the Stoics, he is said to have been equally well versed in mathematics, physics, rhetoric, and poetics. Of the beginning of Amyrutzes' connection with the Turkish court Critoboulos says, in the year 1461, that Muhammad,

who himself is well trained in philosophy, sent for Amyrutzes and, after a thorough examination as to his general instruction and his philosophical knowledge, accorded him an honorable position at court and the rare privilege of coming into his presence and of proposing to him the opinions of the ancients, especially philosophical problems and their resolution.[37]

Critoboulos had earlier reported, in the summer of 1455, that the sultan, weary with campaigning,

gave himself up to the study of philosophy, as much to that of the Arabs and Persians as to that of the Hellenes. Daily he talked with the leaders and masters of thought, of whom there were not a few with whom he had surrounded himself and with whom he was accustomed to make his studies and researches in philosophy and in the dogmas of this science; above all he was pleased with those of the Peripatetics and Stoics. In the course of a study of the works of Ptolemy, who, both as scientist and philosopher, expounds the entire world and all that is therein, Muhammad desired that this exposition and the maps which went with it, which were cut and scattered, should be brought together upon one single piece of linen. He therefore charged the philosopher Georges with this task, promising royal honor and reward to one who should depict the entire habited earth upon one map. . . . He also commanded a translation of the entire works of Ptolemy into Arabic.[38]

At intervals there were also resident at Muhammad's court several Italian artists and writers. About the time of the founding of the Palace School and a full score of years before the famous visit of Gentile Bellini to Constantinople, Muhammad was acquainted with the work of the painter and medalist, Matteo de' Pasti of Verona. Desiring to have a portrait made of himself, the sultan asked Signor Sigismond Pandolphe Malatesta to arrange to have de' Pasti come to Constantinople. As a result of this request de' Pasti spent some time at the court and during his stay made several likenesses of the sultan. It was about the year 1474 that Angiolello for a second time took up his residence at the Grand Seraglio. He had previously written an account of the siege of Negropont which is thought to have pleased the sultan very much. Having accompanied Muhammad on his Persian campaign against Shah Uzun-Hasan, he wrote an account of this also, and at the royal behest made a Turkish translation. Writing later in his *Historia turchesca* of the great pleasure which Muhammad took in pictures, Angiolello says, "It was I who wrote to the illustrious government of Venice that they should send one of their best painters to Constantinople, and there was sent Gentile Bellini, a very expert painter, whom Muhammad used to see freely." During the months (1479–80) that Bellini remained at the Turkish court, a third Italian artist, Bartolomeo Bellano, was also resident there. Among the Italian men of letters may be mentioned "the father of modern archaeology," Cyriacus of Ancona, who was attached to the court of Muhammad before the conquest of Constantinople and who accompanied him at the time of his entry into the city; and the Florentine, Francesco Berlinghieri, who dedicated to Muhammad his translation of Ptolemy in Italian rhyme.[39]

During the reign of Muhammad the curriculum of the Palace School is said by Ata to have included courses "in nomadic life and in civilization, in the science of utility, in diplomacy, in the art of war, and in the various 'sciences' and 'arts.'" Incentives offered for excellence in study were the personal approbation of the sultan, rapid promotion to office, and the differential rates of scholarships, or allowances, which were apportioned at this time. The sword-bearers, for example, received fifty *aqchas* a day, other student officers thirty-five, pages of the royal bedchamber twenty, and those of the halls of the Treasury, Commissariat, and Great Hall, eight. In the reign of the son of Muhammad, Bayazid II, the pages of the Great Hall received thirty-one *aqchas* a day.[40] Muhammad is said to have exercised extraordinary vigilance over the staff and the student body, making the rounds of the different halls constantly by day and by night in order to ascertain if the pages were comfortable, and if they performed well the tasks which were assigned to them. To those who completed the full course of study he awarded a diploma with his own seal (*tughra*) attached. In order to insure that the teaching should be of the best quality, Muhammad exercised a strict personal oversight and control over the instruction of the Palace School. If a teacher neglected the performance of his duty, Muhammad would address a personal letter of admonition to him and would recommend him to return to his teaching. In a case of continued neglect, he sometimes imprisoned the offender or, in a case of flagrant offense, banished him from the court, although he was accustomed to exercise great indulgence towards men of letters, especially poets.[41]

It is stated by Ata that to meet the increasing needs of the school Muhammad twice enlarged his first palace, the Old Palace (*Eski Saray*), which, immediately following the conquest of Constantinople, he had built upon the third hill of the city, and that its further growth was the main reason for the transfer of his official residence to Seraglio Point.[42] If the general plan of Muhammad's new palace was similar to that of the present Grand Seraglio, as seems almost certain,[43] the school, as the inevitable consequence of the personal services which the pages and the white eunuchs performed for the sultan, would have occupied a situation then, as it does now, in the third court; and, in conformity with every tradition which was followed throughout the later history of the school, there would have been a hall which served as combined classroom and dormitory for each of the separate schools. Muhammad is said to have built also a large library for the school and a hospital with bath for the staff.[44]

There exists, fortunately, the very early account of the Palace School by Angiolello. This description has

all the simplicity and crudeness of a primitive as compared with a work of art of the High Renaissance, but
the rudiments of the school are there. Beginning with
a description of the duties of the three principal white
eunuchs of the Grand Seraglio — the chief eunuch, the
head treasurer, and the head commissary, who were the
disciplinary officers of the school — Angiolello continues
as follows:

Each of these eunuchs has about one hundred pages under
him, all slaves of various nationalities, each of whom has an
allowance of eight aspres,* together with gifts and horses,
from the Great Turk. In addition there are about twenty
youths who attend the Great Turk, that is to say, the apartment where he dwells, and these attendants receive twenty
aspres a day, besides numerous gifts. There are also twenty
other eunuchs who serve as messengers to the three chief
eunuchs, because the Great Turk does not desire that anyone within the palace should converse with the guards who
are at the palace gates, or with any other person outside the
palace. And when anyone within the palace wishes to buy
something legitimate, he must give the order to one of these
twenty eunuchs and they are obliged to take the money to
the guards who are stationed at the first gate, and to order
them to make the desired purchase or to perform any other
service. These guards must execute faithfully the orders.
These twenty eunuchs get eight aspres a day, with gifts and
horses. And when the place of one of the three chief eunuchs
falls vacant, the Great Turk promotes one of the twenty to
his place.

But I have to remark that all those [pages] who are in the
service of the Great Turk, who are about three hundred and
forty in number,[45] all alike are sons of Christians, in part
taken in military expeditions into foreign countries and in
part drawn from his own subjects. The Great Turk takes into

* A European corruption of the Greek equivalent of *aqcha*.

his service only young men who are eighteen years of age, or thereabouts. In the Grand Seraglio there are two permanent teachers, old masters of good life who are required to teach the pages to read; also they instruct them in the rites and ceremonies of the Moslem law. In accordance as they conduct themselves, the pages are assigned to the offices of the royal household to attend upon the Great Turk, and after they have been in his service a certain time, when in the opinion of the lord he can trust them, he sends them out of the palace with salaries which are increased as he thinks fitting. And when they have made a good record they are promoted from one rank to another and increased in dignities and in salaries; thus the greater part of the lords, captains, and great men who are in the service of the Great Turk receive their education in the royal palace, as has already been said, and there are few of them who do not accomplish their duties, because they are rewarded for the smallest service to their lord, and also because they are punished for the smallest fault.[46]

Angiolello's designation of the youths in attendance upon the sultan in the royal bedchamber as *cameriere* (attendants), whereas all the other youths in the palace service are referred to as pages, would seem to imply that while the halls of the Treasury and the Commissariat already existed, the Hall of the Royal Bedchamber had not yet been formally instituted as an *oda*, or corps, at the time when the *Historia turchesca* was written. This supposition is borne out by the assertion of Ata that sometime after the transfer to the Grand Seraglio, when Muhammad called "a great deliberative assembly" of the pages of the Treasury and Commissariat in order to discuss the organization and the future development of the Palace School, no mention was made of the Hall of the Royal Bedchamber. This supposition is further supported by the Code of Laws of

Muhammad II (*Qanunname-yi . . . Muhammad Khan*), which there is good reason to believe was not framed until near the end of the reign, most probably between the years 1477 and 1481,[47] the year of Muhammad's death. In that code the number of pages attendant upon the royal person had been increased and the formal organization of an additional hall is recorded as follows:

There has been formed a Hall of the Royal Bedchamber [*Khas Oda*] which has thirty-two pages and four officers. The first of these is the Sword-bearer [*Silahdar*], the second is Master of the Horse [*Rikiabdar*], and the third is Master of the Wardrobe [*Choqadar*], and the fourth is Master of the Turban [*Tulbend Oghlani*]. The Sword-bearer has charge of the discipline of the Novices [*Ajemi-oghlanlar*], and he has also been appointed Head Gatekeeper of the Palace [*Qapuji Bashi*]. . . . The First Officer of the Royal Bedchamber [*Oda Bashi*] has been given charge of all the royal pages.[48]

According to the historian Ali Efendi (1541–1599) and to palace tradition, Muhammad established two other halls: the Great Hall or *Buyuk Oda*, and the Small Hall or *Kuchuk Oda*, which served the purpose of preparatory schools to the three schools of vocational training. The same historian's detailed estimate of the number of pages in each of the halls of the Palace School during the reign of Muhammad differs so widely from that of the contemporary historian, Angiolello, and altogether his picture of the school is so finished as to suggest that, after the manner of early historians, he gives not an authentic description of the school in an earlier period but a reflection of the school as it existed in his own time. In view also of the fact that the two preparatory schools were almost identical as to organization, curriculum, and purpose, it seems unlikely that more than one of these was founded by Muhammad. The Great Hall, which was at first called the New Hall, is known on the authority of Giovanni Antonio Menavino, a page of Genoese origin who was in the palace service for nearly a decade, to have been in existence during the reigns of Bayazid II and Selim I,[49] Muhammad's son and grandson, and therefore may have been in existence during the reign of Muhammad himself. In view of the fact that the Small Hall is not mentioned in the list of halls by Menavino, who left the palace service about 1514, and that no mention of it has been found prior to that by the Venetian *bailo*, Navagero, in 1553,[50] it seems likely that the Small Hall was added to the Palace School at the time of the marked increase in the number of pages by Suleiman the Magnificent, and that it was in consequence of the building of this hall that the name of the older hall was changed from the New Hall to the Great Hall.

The development of the Palace School from the embryo school of princes of Murad II into the military school of state of the powerful Ottoman Empire, which continued to exist and to function effectively along the same general lines for three and a half centuries, takes rank in the history of education as an achievement of a very high order. In working out a scheme for the curriculum of his school Muhammad does not appear to have followed slavishly any known models, but to have created a system of education along new lines — extra-constitutional lines, in fact. In the theocracy of Islam, as has already been pointed out, no systematic provision for higher education existed outside the body of the Ulema, and the only precedents for a school of statecraft were those founded on the model of the Nizamiyah, which had ceased to exist. Yet, while the organization and discipline of the school and the requirement of manual training were characteristically Turkish, the curriculum as later developed, in its unique combination of the study of the liberal arts with systematic physical training, resembles closely the academy of Plato, as Professor Lybyer has pointed out. Certain elements in particular would appear to have been derived from *The Republic*: the early division into intellectuals and artisans, as seen in the Inner and Outer services of the Grand Seraglio, the systematic and long-continued training of the body, the emphasis upon music, including choral music, the freedom allowed in the choice of subjects in accordance with the natural bent of the individual student, *et çetera*. There would also seem to be a suggestion of Renaissance influence upon Muhammad himself in the condemnation by Muhammad's own son, Bayazid II, of his father's tendencies and tastes, as reported by Angiolello. He relates that while Gentile Bellini was in the Turkish service — a situation that, in view of the Moslem attitude towards the representation of life in art, was in itself unorthodox — Muhammad caused him to make many portraits and pictures of subjects of a lascivious character (*massime di cose di lussuria*),

and some of these last were so beautiful that he caused a great number of them to be hung in his palace. When Bayazid succeeded his father, he immediately caused these paintings to be sold in the bazaars, and many of them were bought by our [Venetian] merchants. The same Bayazid was wont to say that his father was *prone* [?] and that he did not believe in the Prophet Muhammad, and such, it would seem, was in effect, the truth. For this same reason everyone says that this Muhammad did not believe in any faith.[51]

Among modern Turkish historians a popular interpretation of the character and career of Muhammad the Conqueror is that, a liberal by nature, he fell greatly under the influence of Byzantine culture, and thus became the exponent among Ottoman Turks of European, in particular Hellenic, civilization, as was Selim I (1512–1520) of Asiatic civilization and Arab religious fanaticism. There would seem to be some grounds for this opinion in the curriculum of the Palace School.

In addition to the mother school of the Grand Seraglio, the palace system of education was presently expanded by the addition of three auxiliary, or outside, preparatory schools, and a fourth vocational school. Following the removal of the capital to Constantinople, Adrianople had been transformed into a summer palace and remained the favorite summer residence of the Turkish sultans until the development of the Sweet Waters of Europe by Ahmed III at the beginning of the eighteenth century. For this reason a large corps of pages continued to be maintained in the Adrianople palace, and it seems likely that the school for pages which was evolved there, the first of the auxiliary schools, was the natural result of the attempt to supply these pages with systematic instruction in line with that received by the pages of the Grand Seraglio. In the reign of Bayazid II, the palace system of schools was further expanded by the addition of a second auxiliary school, the Galata *Saray*, founded upon the same site as the present school of that name, which is the un-broken continuation of the old. Like the Adrianople school, it prepared for entrance into the Great Hall and the Small Hall of the Grand Seraglio, and it was here, at least during a part of its history, that the youngest of the page recruits were segregated.[52] The famous grand vizir under Suleiman the Magnificent, Ibrahim Pasha, founded a third auxiliary school, which was es-pecially "affected to" tribute children from Bosnia and Albania.[53] This school, which was adjacent to the Hippodrome, and bore the name of its founder, became the largest of the five preparatory schools. The fourth hall of vocational training, the Hall of the Expeditionary Force (*Seferli Oda*), the pages of which accompanied the sultan and furnished military music and laundered the royal linen whenever he quitted the Grand Seraglio, was added by Ahmed I (1603–1617).[54] This hall was the ninth and last unit of the Palace School and the sixth within the Grand Seraglio.

CHAPTER II

PLAN OF THE BUILDINGS

THE great imperial palace built by Muhammad the Conqueror and known among Europeans as the Grand
Seraglio stands on Seraglio Point, a high peninsula ex-
tending between the Sea of Marmora and the Golden
Horn. This palace formerly consisted of three great
courts, aligned one after the other along the axis of the
first hill of New Rome and connected by a series of three
great gates. From the middle of the sixteenth century
until the present time — and probably from the first
founding of the Grand Seraglio, if Luigi Bassano da
Zara [1] and Pierre Gilles [2] are correct in their statements that the palace which they knew and described
was the original palace built by Muhammad II — the
buildings of the Palace School, together with the Imperial Treasury, the Pavilion of the Holy Mantle, and
the Privy Commissariat, to all of which the royal pages
and the white eunuchs were attached, have formed the
quadrangle of the third court, serving the purpose of a
vestibule, or antechamber, to the House of Felicity. At
the height of its development the school consisted of a
separate hall, or joint dormitory and recitation building,
for each of the six schools; a conservatory of music,
which was a building for instruction and for practice
without dormitory accommodation; the mosque of the
Palace School [3] and a smaller mosque restricted to the
students of the Great Hall; a common bath for staff

and students, known as the Bath of Selim II; a common room for the faculty and staff; [4] and four separate apartments, or offices, for the four highest officials of the school administration. With the exceptions only of the field for archery and dart practice (*jerid meydani*) in the gardens of the Outer Palace, the school infirmary in the first court, and the kitchens in the second, there were no buildings of the school outside the third court.

In the early period the relative positions of the different schools deviated somewhat from those in the present palace as they are given in the excellent plan published in 1936 by the direction of the *Topqapu* Museum.* The Hall of the Royal Bedchamber stood in the western corner of what may be called the fourth court or inner garden, occupying the intervening space between the Pavilion of the Holy Mantle, the Baghdad Kiushk, and the Boxwood Garden. It was formerly connected with the sultan's apartment, or royal *selamlik*, by a door and a staircase which, according to an inscription still to be seen near the doorway, was closed in 960 A.H. (1552/3) by order of the sultan and the first officer of the royal bedchamber. The remains of this ancient building, now referred to as the "Old Hall of the Royal Bedchamber" (*Eski Khas Oda*), may be reached through a small doorway underneath the Erivan Kiushk; and the tall foundation arches which once supported it may be seen beneath the marble terrace which connects the Kiushk of Circumcision with the Baghdad Kiushk. The original positions of the Great and Small halls also, which have today entirely disappeared, differed considerably from

* The Grand Seraglio in 1924 became the *Topqapu* Museum.

those which they later occupied. The Great Hall is said
to have occupied at first the present position of the Hall
of the Commissariat, and the Small Hall, which, as has
been previously said, was not built until the reign of
Ahmed I, that of the present Hall of the Expeditionary
Force. The first Hall of the Treasury is believed to have
been in its present place.[5] No information appears to
be available concerning the original site of the Hall of
the Commissariat.

The *Serai enderum* [sic], *cioè, Penetrale dell' Seraglio
detto nuovo dei G. S^ri e Re Ottomani, la descrittione del
loro vivere e costumi, et altri essercitii* (1665) of Albert
Bobovi (Bobowski or Bobrowsky), the fullest and most
authoritative account of the Palace School which has
been brought to light in the course of the present study,
contains a plan which purports to show the palace as it
was previous to 1665; it is, indeed, the only known plan
of the palace prior to the great fire of 1664/5. Bobovi,
a Pole in origin, who was taken captive by the Tatars
and sold by them to Turkish slave dealers, ultimately
passing into the possession of the sultan, was a "music
page" in the Palace School for nineteen years and, for
a time, first dragoman of the Porte. Finally dismissed
from the royal service because of such "an inordinate
fondness for wine that his heart could be won at any
time by a flask of it," and unable to obtain employment
of any kind, he abjured Islam, discarded his Turkish
pseudonym of Ali Bey, and turned to account his intimate knowledge of the Palace School by writing the
Serai Enderum, a treatise written in the form of a key
to the plan, chiefly of the third court, and designed,
it is believed, for private circulation in manuscript

"among the representatives of the foreign powers in Constantinople and among the princes of Europe."

The *Serai Enderum* and the accompanying plan have a curious history. It is known that Bobovi wrote the original in Italian, the diplomatic language of the period. Four versions have been found, three containing the plan: an Italian manuscript in the Harleian Collection of the British Museum dated Pera, May 10, 1665, which, to judge from a comparison of the script with that of Bobovi's signature (which is believed to be authentic) to his translation of the Gospel of St. John, now in the library of the Royal University of Leyden, is almost certainly not the original manuscript of the author;[6] second, an anonymous French translation under the title, *Mémoires sur les Turcs*, a manuscript in the Count Paul Riant Collection of Harvard University dated November 10, 1666, which does not appear ever to have been published; and a German translation by Nicholas Brenner, a Swabian and quartermaster of the imperial Poischen (?) regiment of infantry, which was "made by candlelight in the gloomy fortress of the Seven Towers in Constantinople" and published in Vienna in 1667. Only three copies of the German translation are known to be extant, one in the Riant Collection, and two in the National Library in Vienna. A fourth version, in Italian, appeared in the miscellany of Cornelius Magnus, *Quanto di piu curioso turchi*, published in Parma in 1679, and in successive reprints of the same in 1682, 1685, and 1692, all without the plan. In explanation the editor says that, after years of fruitless search and waiting, he has been unable to obtain a copy of the plan and believes it to be irretrievably lost; he has, however, decided to publish the key without the plan, for the reason that the work "contains much new material," and that "even those most familiar with the royal palace believe it to be a truthful and exact account of those things which appear to be monstrously exaggerated." This fourth text seems soon to have been lost sight of, owing partly to the unintelligibility of much of it without the plan and partly to its inclusion in the heterogeneous material of a miscellany. It also seems likely that one of these versions of the *Serai Enderum*, or Bobovi in person, was the chief source of the seven chapters on the Grand Seraglio in Rycaut's *Present State of the Ottoman Empire* (1668). Concerning his sources, Rycaut says in his Epistle to the Reader that "the Relation of the Seraglio, and Education of their Youth, with divers other matters of Custome and Rule, were transmitted to me by several Sober Persons, trained up in the best education of the Turkish Learning; and *particularly by an understanding Polonian who had spent nineteen years in the Ottoman Court.*" Again, at the conclusion of the section on the Grand Seraglio, he repeats that he obtained his information chiefly *"from the mouth of one who had spent nineteen years in the Schools of the Seraglio."* That the person who is described was Bobovi seems evident, not only from the exactness of the description, but also from the fact that the Italian and French manuscripts of the *Serai Enderum* are dated Constantinople, 1665 and 1666 respectively, and that Rycaut spent the six years from 1661 to 1667 in Constantinople as a member of the embassy of Heneage Finch, Earl of Winchelsea. He could therefore have known Albert Bobovi after his dismissal from the Grand Seraglio and about the time that the *Serai Enderum* was composed.

There exists much uncertainty concerning the relation of these four copies of the Bobovi treatise to a common source, and a grave doubt concerning the authenticity of the surviving plans. In all three versions of the plan, it is not the first great gate of the palace which is called the Imperial Gate (*Bab-i Humayun*), but the entrance to the third court, the correct appellation of which is the Gate of Felicity (*Bab as-Saadet*). It seems impossible that anyone with any knowledge of Constantinople could have made so egregious a blunder in regard to one of the best-known and most striking features of the city. There are also some variations in the different plans as to the allocation of several separate buildings, suites, and rooms. On the other hand Bobovi's assertion that he spent nineteen years as a page in the Grand Seraglio seems placed beyond question both by external evidence, such as that of Cornelius Magnus, and by the first-hand character of the information concerning the school contained in the treatise. The simplest and most obvious explanation, namely that the original plan was in reality lost and destroyed, as Cornelius Magnus concluded, and that some copyist made a not entirely satisfactory plan from the text, which later copyists have each altered somewhat, does not fully explain the enigma, since all the copies in question seem to have been made in Constantinople while Bobovi was still alive and presumably within reach.

In spite of such doubts and discrepancies, however, the plans, as measured by the text of the treatise and all available contemporary data, appear to be generally accurate, and have historical interest on account of the changes made in the palace after the fires of 1664/5 and 1856/7. With due allowance for poor draftmanship and proportioning, the relative positions of the Hall of the Royal Bedchamber, the *selamlik*, and the harem are accurate, as are also those of the Imperial Treasury and the Bath of Selim II. There is no separate mention of the Pavilion of the Holy Mantle, but the Hall of the Royal Bedchamber was sometimes used as a covering term for both. The Great Hall and the Small Hall, both of which, as has already been said, have disappeared from the present palace, occupied corresponding positions immediately to the right and left of the entrance to the third court (Plan I, 4, 6),[7] where now stand the quarters of the white eunuchs and the suite of the chief white eunuch. The Privy Commissariat, the Hall of the Commissariat, and the Hall of the Treasury were on the side of the court opposite the third gate in the order given from left to right (Plan I, 29, 27, 25); in the present palace the Privy Commissariat has disappeared and the order of the two halls has been reversed. So accurate is the plan of the third court in some minor details which can still be checked, as in the positions of the Furnace of the Bath (Plan I, 19) and the Gate of the Bird-Cage (Plan I, 38), that one is inclined to believe that it may possibly be accurate also in those parts which cannot be verified. A particularly valuable feature in all three copies is the detailed plan of the school infirmary, which was situated immediately to the right of the entrance of the first court, for the reason that the infirmary has since completely disappeared and no other plan is known to exist which would throw light on the

I. Plan of the Grand Seraglio of Stambul

KEY

1. Imperial Gate
2. Gate of the Chief Black Eunuch
3. Room of the Head Gatekeeper
4. Dormitory of the Pages of the Great Hall
5. Sand Gate (Rear Gate of the Great Hall)
6. Small Hall
7. Rear Door of the Small Hall
8. Door of the Women's Dormitory opening into Court B
9. Room of the Chief Black Eunuch
10. Place where the Pages and Eunuchs perform their Ablutions
11. Door of the Small Hall opening into the Third Court
12. Great Gate opposite the Imperial Gate
13. Gate of the Great Hall opening into Court F
14. Suite of the Palace Steward
15. Place where the Negroes wash the vessels and spoons and the Stokers are instructed in Military Exercises
16. Designation omitted
17. Designation omitted
18. Common Room of the Eunuchs and the Nine Masters of Petitions
19. Furnace of the Bath and Room of the Stokers
20. Hall of the Expeditionary Force
21. Bath of Selim II
22. Conservatory of Music
23. Arcade in front of the Imperial Treasury
24. Imperial Treasury
25. Hall of the Imperial Treasury
26. Station of the Master Artisans of the Wardrobe and of the Silverware
27. Hall of the Privy Commissariat
28. Office of the Steward of the Privy Commissariat
29. Office of the Privy Commissary
30. Watchman's Kiushk
31. Hall of the Pages of the Royal Bedchamber
32. Arcade in front of the Hall of the Royal Bedchamber
33. Royal *Selamlik* (between the Royal Harem and the Hall of the Pages of the Royal Bedchamber)
34. Long Room of the Royal Favorites (*Khasekis*)
35. Office of the Sword-bearer
36. Imperial Mosque
37. Office of the Master of the Wardrobe
38. Vestibule of the Bird-cage, or Aviary, between the Apartments of the Pages and the Royal Harem
39. Inner Door of the Royal Harem
40. Pool with large Fountain
41. Hall of Falconers
41h. Little Room of the Head Falconer
42. Throne Room for the Reception of Ambassadors
43. Arcade of the Throne Room
A. [Second Court]
B. [Court of the Queen-mother]
C. Small Mosque (*Mesjid*) to which the Pages of the Great Hall go four times daily to say their prayers
D. Retreat of the Mutes
44. Dormitory of the Halberdiers-with-Tresses
45. The Divan in which meet the High Judges of the Empire, the Grand Vizir, etc.
46. Arcade where attend the Defendants, Notaries, and other Inferior Officers of the Divan
47. Confectionery Kitchens
48. General Kitchens
49. Section of the Palace Gardens
50. Infirmary of the Palace School
51. Room of the Superintendent of the Infirmary

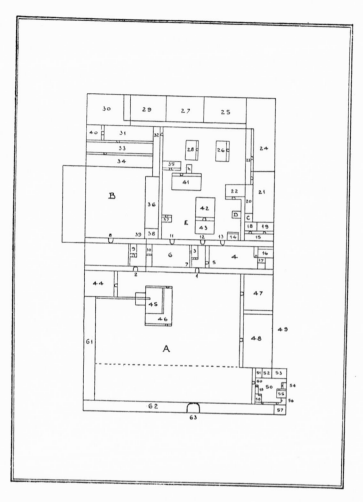

52. Dormitory of the old Slave Laundresses attached to the Infirmary

53. Infirmary of the Pages of the Royal Bedchamber and of the Masters of Petitions

54. Infirmary of the Pages of the Treasury and of the Privy Commissariat

55. Infirmary of the Pages of the Great Hall

56. Infirmary of the Pages of the Expeditionary Force

57. Infirmary of the Pages of the Small Hall

58. Infirmary Bath

59. Infirmary of the Eunuchs

60. Entrance to the Infirmary

61. Ward of the Infirmary formerly assigned to the Cavaliers (*Jindis*)

62. Room of the Messengers, or Porters, in attendance upon the Pages

63. First, or Great, Gate of the Palace

position of this building. The Bath of Selim II (Plan I, 21), now a part of the Museum of Chinese Porcelain, was to the rear of the Hall of the Commissariat. Projecting into the quadrangle of the third court were the Conservatory of Music (Plan I, 22) and the offices of the palace steward (Plan I, 14), of the sword-bearer (Plan I, 35), and of the master of the wardrobe (Plan I, 37). The imperial mosque, which, in order that the *mihrab* (a kind of apse in Islamic architecture) may point towards Mecca, today stands in a position diagonal to the northern side of the third court, in the Bobovi plan appears in approximately the same situation, but is aligned with the wall. Entirely detached from the line of the quadrangle, in the open space of the court, stood the Throne-Room-Without, the Hall of the Head Falconer, the Kiushk of the Assistant Treasurer, and the Kiushk of the Chief Commissary. The last three buildings have disappeared, and there remain in the open space of the court only the Throne-Room-Without and the library, which was added later by Ahmed III.

According to the Bobovi text, the plans of the Great and Small halls were similar: each being a great rectangular chamber, that of the Great Hall about eighty feet in length; each having a gallery, which was sometimes used for dormitory space and sometimes to stow away the coffers in which the pages kept their clothing and other personal belongings; [8] and each having a door opening into the narrow passageway between the two halls. The door of the Great Hall which opened immediately into the court (Plan I, 13) was always closed at sunset, while the corresponding door of the Small Hall (Plan I, 11) was not closed until after the return of the pages from attendance at the last prayer of the day in the imperial mosque. The side doors of both halls were closed during the day but were opened after sunset for the passage at intervals of the night-watch. Two pages with snuffers in hand were stationed at each door in order to snuff the tall candles which burned in the halls throughout the night.[9] A third door leading from the Great Hall into the court was known as the Sand Gate, because near this door was the pile of sand with which the pages scoured their metal dishes after each meal. The walls of both halls are said to have been faced with sheets of gold and silver worked in arabesque pattern and studded with innumerable stones, and the vaulted roofs to have been brilliant with the color and glitter of polychrome tile.

The very interesting plan of the Great Hall which is reproduced below is found only in the German transla-tion of the *Serai Enderum*,[10] the blank space left for the plan in the Italian and French manuscripts never hav-ing been filled in.[11] According to this plan, a distin-guishing feature of the Great Hall was the alternation, around the four sides, of fourteen stalls containing ac-commodations for ten students each, with twelve daises upon each of which were stations for two surveillance officers, an old and a young eunuch. The station of the presiding officer at the end of the room (Plan II, 14, 15) is said to have been enclosed in glass.[12] While the gross-ness of the names by which several of these stalls are designated smacks of an army camp or barracks rather than of an official school of state, it should be borne in mind that the omnipresence of certain small plagues in the Orient goes far towards explaining such terminology.

II. Plan of the Great Hall

From the *Serai Enderum* of Albert Bobovi (1667)

KEY

1. Sand Door
2. Stall of the Latest Arrival
3. Formerly the Stall of the Algerian Pages
4. Stall adjacent to the Door
5. Stall infested with Fleas
6. Stall infested with Fleas
7. Stall infested with Lice
8. Station of the First Officer
9. Stall of Stokers
10. Stall of Bathers
11. Stall of Bathers
12. Two-storied Stall, formerly the Dais where the Royal Princes received their appointments to provincial governorships; now the Station of: (*a*) Those who arrange Turbans and keep in order the Clocks and Watches; (*b*) Mutes and Dwarfs
13. Station of Leader of Daily Ritual (Imam)
14. Station of Presiding Officer
15. Station of Presiding Officer

The present halls of the Royal Bedchamber, Treasury, and Commissariat were built during the reign of Sultan Abd ul-Mejid,[13] following the great fire of 1856/7. In general plan these three halls have certain features in common with the fourth vocational hall, the Hall of the Expeditionary Force, which dates from the seventeenth century. The style of all four is characterized by a certain archaic simplicity. Each is a two-storied rectangular building surmounted with barrel vaulting. The Hall of the Expeditionary Force has three vaults — a large central barrel vault pierced by curious domed windows, and two smaller ones to the front and rear, the whole supported by two rows of seven piers each. Each of the four halls has a colonnaded portico roofed with a series of dome units. Like the Hall of the Expeditionary Force, which formerly had a two-storied gallery supported by square beams around four sides of the room,[14] the halls of the Royal Bedchamber and Treasury have second-story galleries, as had also the Hall of the Commissariat previous to its remodeling.[15] These architectural similarities make it seem likely that a standardized plan for the halls of the Palace School was evolved at an earlier date and that it is this plan which has been perpetuated in the halls of the palace today.[16]

The only detailed description found of the Hall of the Royal Bedchamber as it existed prior to its rebuilding in the nineteenth century is that gleaned by Jean Baptiste Tavernier from two renegade attendants of the Treasury whom he met during the course of his wide travels. Their account was the basis of his *Nouvelle Relation de l'interieur du Serrail du Grand Seigneur*, published in 1675,[17] and later combined with his *Six*

*Voyages . . . through Turky into Persia, and the East
Indies.* According to them the hall consisted of a dormitory for the pages of the royal bedchamber opening
directly upon the third court; and three private rooms
or offices belonging to the first three officers of the hall,
the sword bearer, the master of the wardrobe, and the
master of the horse.[18] The walls of the dormitory are
said to have been bare save for several square gilt tablets
upon the right-hand wall, and an inscription, *La Illa
He Illa* (*La Ilaha illa 'llah*, There is no God but Allah),
in gold lettering over the doorway. At each of the corners was a medallion of black marble inscribed with
the names of the Companions of the Prophet. Ranged
around the four sides of the chamber were the beds of
the pages, and in the center was a dais which was the
station of the first officer of the royal bedchamber.

Beyond the Hall of the Royal Bedchamber was a
large domed room with two doors, that on the left hand
leading to a flower garden, and that on the right to the
Pavilion of the Holy Mantle, the repository of the holy
relics of the Prophet which Selim I brought from Egypt
at the time of his conquest of that country and the
assumption of the caliphate. The domed room, which
apparently served as an anteroom to the Winter Chamber within the Pavilion of the Holy Mantle,* is said to

* At the time of my return to Constantinople in 1928 to complete my
book on the Grand Seraglio, *Beyond the Sublime Porte*, I observed in the
Administration Building of the palace, formerly the Hall of the Commissariat, a Turkish plan of the third court which included a plan of the Pavilion of the Holy Mantle, and showed the position of the coffer containing
the Holy Mantle (Plan III). Although no information could be obtained
concerning the origin of this plan, its general character and the absence in
it of certain features known to have existed earlier than the nineteenth cen-

III. Turkish Plan of the Third
Court from a Plan of the
Grand Seraglio, *ca. 1855*

KEY

1. Gate of Felicity
2. Office of the Slaves (Pages) of
   the First Officer (*Agha*) of
   the Gate of Felicity
3. Palace School
4. Third Ward of the Pages of the
   Imperial Treasury
5. Imperial Treasury
6. Office of the Pages of the Steward of the Imperial Treasury
7. First Ward of the Pages of the
   Imperial Treasury
8. Treasury of the Holy Relics
9. Office of the Holy Mantle
10. Private Ward of the Pages of
    the Holy Mantle
11. Private Mosque of the Pages
    of the First Officers
12. Imperial Library
13. Imperial Throne Room
14. Private Ward of the Pages of
    the First Officers of the Gate
    of Felicity

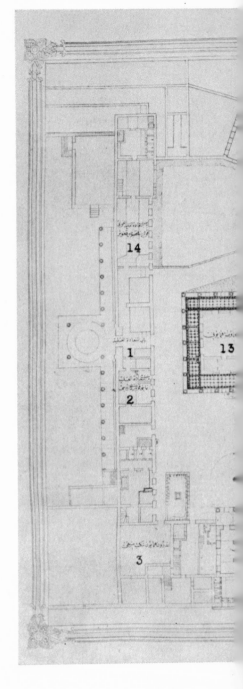

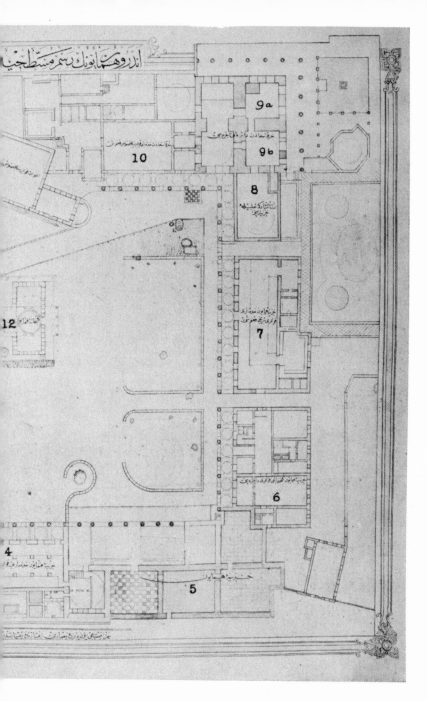

have been particularly large and well lighted.[19] Tavernier gives the following vivid description of it and of the
Winter Chamber:

Adjoyning to the Door of the *Haz-Oda* [Hall of the Royal
Bedchamber], there is a Hall pav'd with a Chequer-work, of
black and white Marble, in the midst whereof there is a Basin
of the same material, but of several colours, out of which
there is an ascent of water four or five feet high. That water
is receiv'd into a second Basin, made in the form of a Scallop-
shell, out of which it falls again into a third, much larger than
the two precedent ones. The upper-part of the Hall is built
Domo-wise, having therein some Windows, which give it
light, and a certain piece of dull painting is all the Ornament
of its Walls. At your entrance into the Hall, you see two
Doors, one on the right hand, the other, on the left. That on
the left conducts to a Flower-Garden; and the other is the
door of a Chamber, into which the Grand Seignor comes sometimes, in the Winter-season.

This Chamber is one of the most sumptuous of any in the
Seraglio. It's arched Roof is divided into a great number of
little Cells, Triangle-wise, distinguish'd by two little filets of
Gold, with a green streak in the midst, and out of every
Angle, there juts somewhat like the bottom of a Lamp, ex-
cellently well gilt. Though the Walls are of a curious white
Marble, yet there is a delicate piece of Wainscotage, of about
the height of a man's waste, carried quite round the Room,
and the rich Carpets, upon which you walk, deprive your
sight of the large squares of Marble, of several colours, where-
with the Floor is embellish'd. Of a great number of Cushions,
which are plac'd along the Walls, some are embroider'd with

tury and the close correspondence of others to the present arrangement of
the court would seem to indicate that it was probably the architect's plan
for the restoration which followed the fire of 1856/7. So far as I was able
to ascertain, it was the only plan of the pavilion in existence at that time.
It was first published in *Beyond the Sublime Porte* in 1931, and is reproduced
here by the courtesy of the Yale University Press.

Pearls, and precious Stones, and set there only for ostentation; the others, which are for service, are cover'd with Gold,
or Silver-Brokadoes, and other costly Stuffs. At one of the
corners of the Chamber, there is a little Field-bed, about
two feet in height, embroider'd all over, the Counterpane,
the Cushions, and the Quilt; and that Embroidery is all of
Pearls, Rubies, and Emeralds. But when the Grand Seignor
is to come into that Chamber, they take away the Counterpane and Cushions which are less fit for Service than for
Ornament, and they bring in others of quilted or tufted Velvet, or Satin, upon which the Grand Seignor may more con-
veniently repose himself.

Towards the feet of the said Bed, there is a kind of Neech
made within the very Wall, in which there is a little Ebony
Box, about a half a foot square, and in that is locked up
Mahomet's Seal. . . . Within the same Chamber, and adjoyning to the place, where the Seal is kept, there is another Box
or Coffer, of a larger size, cover'd with a Carpet of green Velvet, with a great fringe of Gold and Silver, wherein is kept
Mahomet's Hirka [*Mantle*].[20]

The rooms of the master of the wardrobe and of the
master of the horse were small and dark. The room of
the sword-bearer, situated between the Hall of the
Royal Bedchamber and the Hall of the Falconers, was
decorated in a similar style, but much more richly. The
walls were paneled with white marble richly carved and
painted in gold and azure. At one side was a dais three
feet high, which was covered with rich silken carpets
and cushions and fenced in by a green and gold balus-
trade. Suspended above the dais were the swords and
sabers carried by the sword-bearer when he appeared in
public with the sultan.[21]

In its present restored condition, the Hall of the Royal
Bedchamber includes, in addition to the usual large

dormitory with gallery, two private rooms separated by a passageway leading to the Pavilion of the Holy Mantle; a suite for the first officer of the royal bedchamber; and an interesting common room known as the Green Room. This room contains the remains of a fine mosaic pavement, and a landscape fresco of a surprisingly romantic character — purling stream, floating lilies, wooded banks, and anemone — said to be by one Ferid Bey. In the court to the rear of the building leading to the Pavilion of the Holy Mantle are the ruins of an ancient infirmary which was once attached to this hall.

The present Imperial Treasury consists of a square domed chamber entered directly from the third court; a communicating chamber with flat ceiling to the left of that; and several subterranean vaults, said by the palace curators to be three in number, the stairways to which are reached through the two small doors, the one in the extreme right-hand corner of the domed chamber and the second in the extreme left-hand corner of the communicating chamber. These vaults are lighted by means of the eight Gothic-like windows between the stationary buttresses which may be seen from the Marmora side of the palace. The date of the present Treasury is not known, but the general style of the architecture — the immensely thick walls, the use of squinches to support the dome, the wall niches, the portico and the great stationary buttresses of the foundation — bears so close a resemblance to that of the adjoining dressing room of Selim II as to suggest that the two buildings are in reality one edifice. The building to the left of the Treasury, which, viewed from the Marmora side of the palace, shows four great arched

windows two stories or more in height, was built by
Mahmud II (1808–1839) and is known as the Ambassadors' Treasury, presumably for the reason that it was
the repository for the plate which was used at the reception of ambassadors.

The visitor to the present Hall of the Treasury sees
only a bare rectangular chamber with an upper gallery.
But the interior of the hall, as described to Tavernier,
was exceedingly rich.

That [the Hall] of the Pages of the Treasury, is hard by
the Kilar, and begins with a Gallery, pav'd with square pieces
of Marble, of different colours, sustain'd by eight Pillars of
the same material, and whereof the sides and the roof are
painted with all sorts of flowers, in Gold and Azure. That
Gallery is open on the one side, and on the other side in the
midst of it, the door leading into the Apartment of the Pages,
with three great Windows on the right hand, and as many on
the left: And 'tis there that the six most elderly of the Pages
of the Treasury have their residence night and day.

From that door, along a walk pav'd with white Marble
stones, very large ones, about fifteen paces in length, and
five in breadth, you come to another Portal of the same material, sustain'd by two Pillars of black Marble; over the said
Portal, there may be read these words, which are ordinary
enough in the mouths of the *Turks*, and which I have expli-
cation elsewhere; *La Illahe' Illa Alla, Muhammed Resoul
Alla*. It gives entrance into a long Hall, where there may be
seen on both sides a Seat, or Scaffold, a foot and a half in
height, and between seven and eight in breadth. Every
Page has but four feet in breadth for his reposing place, as
well by day, as by night: And for their Beds, they are permitted to have under them only a Woolen Coverlet, four
times doubled, which serves them for a Quilt, and over that
they ordinarily have one of Gold or Silver-Brockado, or some
other sumptuous Silk-stuff; and in the Winter time, they

are permitted to have three of them. They are not to have
their Coverlets all of Wooll, which would be so much warmer,
because it would not be a decent sight for the Grand Seignor,
when he comes ever and anon, in the night time, pretending
indeed as if he would surprize them, and see how they demean
themselves, but in effect, sometimes to cover lewd designs.
'Tis between these Coverlets that the Pages take their repose, having their Wast-coat and Drawers on; for there is no
talk of any other kind of Linnen, either in *Turkey*, or any
part of the East; and whether it be Winter or Summer, they
alwaies lay themselves down to sleep, half clad, without any
Great Ceremony.

Over the Beds of the Pages, there is a Gallery, which goes
quite round the Hall, and is sustain'd by Pillars of Wood,
painted all over with red varnish, and there they have their
Coffers. . . . At one of the ends of the Hall, there is a Door,
which conducts you to the Fountaines, where those that have
their dependance on the Treasury go and wash, when they
are call'd to their Devotions. There are seven Copper Cocks
for that convenience, and as well the pavement, as the Walls,
of that place are of white Marble.[22]

The halls of the Commissariat and of the Expeditionary Force have undergone extensive changes. The
former has been converted into an office building for the
Museum administration. The Hall of the Expeditionary
Force formerly extended about twenty feet beyond the
line of the present colonnade, to the point where the
ancient foundation may still be traced, but was reduced
to its present size by Sultan Abd ul-Mejid.[23] Together
with the dressing room of the Bath of Selim II to the
rear, with which it is connected by a central doorway,[24]
it is now used as a museum for the large and rare collection of celadon amassed by the sultans from an early
date. This collection is said to have been discovered

in the Inner Treasury and to have been removed here
at the time of the Kaiser's last visit to Constantinople.

Only six officials of the Palace School — the chief
white eunuch, who was at one and the same time head
of the Inner Service of the Grand Seraglio and director
of the Palace School; the palace steward, who was its
assistant-director, quartermaster, and paymaster; the
head treasurer, the assistant treasurer, the chief commissary, and the grand falconer — had separate apartments, all other white eunuchs being quartered in the
halls of the pages to which they were assigned as surveillance officers.[25] In the plan of the Bobovi manuscript the suite of the chief white eunuch is situated
immediately to the left of the Gate of Felicity (Plan
III, 3). This suite is said to have consisted of an anteroom with a fountain, a reception room richly decorated
with carved and gilded woodwork, a bedroom, and a
room for servants.[26] Since the fire of 1856/7 and the
subsequent restoration of the wings to the right and left
of the Gate of Felicity by Sultan Abd ul-Mejid, this
suite occupies the right wing. The left wing, according
to Abd ur-Rahman Sherif Efendi, who, in a series of
eight articles in the *Journal of the Turkish Historical
Society (Tarikh-i Osmani Enjumeni Mejmuasi)*, published in 1913 the first account of the Grand Seraglio
after the opening of the forbidden portions, once contained the apartment of the head treasurer.[27] As late
as 1928 it was actually occupied by the few remaining
members of the corps of white eunuchs still retained in
the palace. The only portions of the two wings which
antedate the restoration by Abd ul-Mejid are the ancient fireplace in the right wing, and the fountain in the

small courtyard of the left wing, which bears the date
1180 A.H. (1766/7).

The office of the palace steward stood to the right of
the Gate of Felicity, adjoining the small mosque of the
Great Hall, and consisted of two rooms: a reception
room and an inner office (Plan III, 14). Both were
fitted with small coffers in which was stored the cash
for the payroll of the Palace School, and with cabinets
and chests for the various garments, textiles, and other
accessories of the wardrobe which were also distributed
to the pages and eunuchs from this office. The walls
of the reception room were paneled with white marble
carved in gilded arabesque.

The office of the steward of the Treasury (*Khazineh-yi
Ketkhuda*), who was also the first officer of the hall of
the pages of the Treasury and in that capacity was required to sleep in the Hall of the Treasury, was in the
kiushk (Plan III, 26) which stood in a detached position in the angle of the court between this hall and the
Treasury. It was in this kiushk that he gave out and
received the work of the goldsmiths, silversmiths,
tailors, and other artisans who were in the employ of
the Treasury.[28]

The Kiushk of the Chief Commissary was situated in
a position to the left of the court (Plan III, 28) corresponding to that of the steward of the Treasury on the
right. This kiushk also had two rooms: a large outer
one which served as a receiving room for the Privy Commissariat, and to the right of that, a smaller one fashioned after the manner of a vault, in which were stored
the plate, porcelain, and glass in current use in the
royal *selamlik* and harem.[29]

The suite of the grand falconer, which stood directly in front of the Kiushk of the Chief Commissary, consisted of two rooms, and was one of the most elaborately decorated in the palace. The walls were richly wainscoted and tiled, the ceilings painted and gilded, and the floors paved with black and white marble. The divans and cushions were covered with richest velvet, satin, and brocade.[30]

The large bath built by Selim II (1566–1574) and called by his name, which was situated to the rear of the Hall of the Expeditionary Force and adjacent to the Imperial Treasury, included accommodations for the entire personnel of the Palace School and a private bath for the sultan, the so-called "dressing room of Selim II." Besides the royal bath the establishment is said to have included two separate baths for the officials of the school; a bath for the pages of the royal bedchamber; a large common bath for the pages of the remaining halls; a "winter dressing room"; a large drying room which was used as a dressing room in summer; several rest rooms for the bath attendants [31] and barbers; and, separated from the remainder of the establishment by a long corridor, a barber shop for the pages of the three upper schools.[32] It is said to have been possible to accommodate as many as three hundred persons in the bath at one time.[33]

In size and general structure the present dressing room of Selim II, which is not shown in the Bobovi plan, but which may be seen in the Turkish plan of the third court, bears a striking resemblance, as has been said, to the adjoining chamber of the Treasury. Both are square chambers roofed over with a dome, and both are lighted by means of two tiers of three windows each in the wall on the Marmora side, the dressing room having a third row of eight windows around the dome, from which immense spheres are said once to have been suspended.

In the walls to the right and left of the entrance to the dressing room are six large niches formerly containing wall fountains; the wall spaces between these niches are faced with blue and white tiles decorated with floral designs in high relief. A fine old pavement of white marble with a central medallion of white and black marble mosaic may very possibly be the original one. The beautiful fountain of "Moorish design" with six jets, which is said to have stood in the center, has completely disappeared. To the right of this chamber, and at the same time to the rear of the Hall of the Expeditionary Force, are several cabinets which were also a part of the sultan's bath. It is said that it was in one of these that Sultan Selim, on the occasion of his first visit shortly after the completion of the building, had the fall that caused his death a few days later.

The bath of the pages of the royal bedchamber is said to have been remarkable for the profuse use of colored marble and semiprecious stones. The walls were faced with red marble inlaid with jasper and agate. There were four floor fountains with large marble basins in the center of the room.[34]

The common bath of the pages of the other halls is described by Tavernier as having been roofed over with an immense dome fitted with

little Glasses made in the fashion of Bells, order'd as Venice-Looking-Glasses . . . the walls are done about with square pieces, that are white and blew, and in every one of them you find a Flower in emboss'd Work, done to the Life, which a man would take for enamell. Little Lamines or Plates of Gold cover the juncture of those square pieces, and there cannot anything be imagin'd more pleasant and divertive than that Chamber is.[35]

The floor, like that of the sultan's bath, was paved in white and black marble. As the capacity of the bath was insufficient to accommodate the entire school at one time, the different corps were each assigned a different day of the week. The petition officers had Friday, the day of honor; other pages of the royal bedchamber, Saturday, and other white eunuchs, Monday; the pages of the Treasury and the falconers, Sunday; the pages of the Expeditionary Force, Tuesday; and the pages of the Great Hall and of the Small Hall respectively, Thursday morning and Thursday afternoon.[36]

The Library of Ahmed III, which was erected in 1718/9 (1131 A.H.) by the sultan whose name it bears, was at first intended for the use of the Palace School only, but was later opened to other members of the palace staff. Curiously situated to the rear of the Throne-Room-Without, it occupies a position which is almost the exact center of the court — a site which is said formerly to have been occupied by a kiushk of Selim II and which, in this instance, was probably selected for the sake of its equal proximity to the various halls.[37] It is a charming small white marble building fashioned, after the classical manner of the *medreseh*, in the form of a Greek cross with a dome over the center supported by columns and with barreled vaulting over the four *liwans*, or wings. The *liwan* facing Seraglio

Point forms a kind of vestibule to the kiushk and on account of the slope of the terrace is furnished with a flight of stairs at either side. While the decorations are somewhat ornate, they are marked by the same refinement of taste which characterizes other buildings of Sultan Ahmed. The walls are finished with bordered panels of blue faïence. The interiors of the dome and vaulted ceilings are pure white, with medallions and other designs in gold tracery; the stalactite-work is also decorated with gold. The large central panes of the three tiers of windows are of clear glass, set in an outer framework of stained glass in scroll or foliated design. The inlaid woodwork of the shutters of the windows and of the double door has a greater proportion of white than the inlay of the earlier period, and is therefore somewhat less pleasing. It is said on Turkish authority that the books and manuscripts this library once contained, which were mostly in Turkish, Arabic, and Persian, but which also included some very rare specimens from Servia, Hungary, and Greece, numbered 3,515 volumes.[38]

CHAPTER III

PERSONNEL AND ORGANIZATION

To UNDERSTAND the system of education evolved in the Palace School it must be kept constantly in mind that for more than three centuries the despotism of the Osmanli dynasty was based almost exclusively upon a deliberate policy of government by a slave class. This method of government [1] would seem to have been developed by the Turkish rulers as a defensive mechanism designed to prevent, by the exclusion of native-born subjects from the government, the rise of an aristocracy of blood or of a hereditary official class. A contemporary opinion was that the Sultan

does not consider birth or fortune in his ministers, but causes himself to be served entirely by those who belong entirely to him, who owe him their nurture and education, and are therefore obliged to employ in his service all that they have of ability and virtue and who render in return and with interest the expense he has been put to for their minds and bodies so much so that he can elevate them without envy and destroy them without danger.[2]

It was even said that the word "slave" currently meant a person "entirely devoted to the will and commandments of the Grand Signor, that is one who does blindly all that he orders, and if it is possible, all that he thinks." [3] In the opinion of Machiavelli as expressed in *The Prince* the Turkish slave system of government had both advantages and disadvantages:

A usurper cannot be called in by the princes of the kingdom, nor can he hope to be assisted in his designs by the revolt of those who the lord has around him . . . for his ministers, being all slaves and bondmen, can only be corrupted with great difficulty, and one can expect but little advantage from them when they have been corrupted, as they cannot carry the people with them, for the reasons assigned. Hence, he who attacks the Turk must bear in mind that he will find him united, and he will have to rely more on his own strength than on the revolt of others; but, if once the Turk has been conquered, and routed in the field in such a way that he cannot replace his armies, there is nothing to fear but the family of the prince, and, this being exterminated, there remains no one to fear, the others having no credit with the people; and as the conqueror did not rely on them before his victory, so he ought not to fear them after it.

The Turkish people themselves, for a time at least, appear to have acquiesced in this theory of government. When, about the middle of the sixteenth century, Guillaume Postel questioned the Turks as to why they preferred to have slaves and foreigners rule them rather than their own people, they gave him "the very philosophical and natural reply that they are better served thus . . . that there is not in the memory of anyone now living a single instance of a Christian thus nourished who has turned traitor." [4]

It must be remembered also, in considering this system of government by a slave class, that slavery in Moslem lands not only was without the stigma that it bore throughout the West but often proved the most direct road to fortune and honor. The teaching of the Prophet that slaves should be treated with kindness and with generosity, that they should be fed and clothed in the same manner as the members of the master's own family, had prevented the Moslem East from attributing to manual labor the degradation which attached to it in the West. This injunction, and the added provision that if for any reason it became impossible to deal with them justly they should be sold or otherwise disposed of in a beneficent manner, had in general greatly alleviated the condition of slaves in Islam. In Moslem lands also it was household slavery that was in general practiced, and not that of the field; and the slave status was regarded not as a permanent one but as accidental and temporary. At the marriage or at the death of an owner or upon occasions of great rejoicing, it was the custom to manumit slaves on a large scale, and even to pension them, in accordance with which custom Muhammad II is said to have freed about forty thousand of his slaves at the conclusion of his campaign against Uzun Hasan of Persia.[5] In substantiation of the statement that slavery was openly recognized as one of the surest routes to honor and fortune may be cited the reply of an Oriental to an Occidental, who was deploring the insecurity of life and property and the many evils of bad government in the Orient: "I acknowledge all that you say to be true. On the other hand in your country under a good government you can nearly always foretell with some degree of certainty what may happen next; in my country the wildest dreams may be realized at any moment. One may be a slave one day, and a grand vizir the next! We Orientals prefer to have it thus."

An illustration of the lightness with which powerful officials regarded the fact of their slave origin and their rapid rise to high fortune is seen in the amusing attitude of Khosrew (Khusrev) Pasha, minister of war under

Sultan Abd ul-Aziz, in a conversation with Sir Adolphus Slade, who, as Mushaver Pasha, was for seventeen years (1849–1866) administrative head of the Turkish navy, toward his own monetary value as compared with that of Halil (Khalil) Pasha. "By birth a Circassian," Admiral Slade writes,

he [Halil] was purchased in the slave market of Constantinople by Khosrew Pasha, who, it is worthy of remark, was bought in the same market. Having no sons, he [Khosrew] finished by adopting the young Halil as "the son of his soul," a common practice in the East, and raised him to the highest offices of state. . . . At this period he [Halil] was about to proceed to St. Petersburgh as ambassador extraordinary. . . . This good fortune of his adopted son gladdened the seraskier [*ser-asker*, or commander-in-chief of the army] and he could not help speaking of it to a Frank in a manner which develops a point in Eastern character.

"It is wonderful," said the old man; "at length Halil is going. God is great. I purchased him; now behold him an *eltchi* [ambassador]. Ah! he was a sweet child, a charming boy; he cost me fifteen hundred piastres."

"Only fifteen hundred!" replied the Frank; "that was not dear for such merit; surely your Excellency cost more?"

"I," said the *seraskier*, "that is quite another thing, truly; I was worth more; I cost my master two thousand five hundred piastres." [6]

During the centuries when the slave system of government was at its height among the Ottoman Turks, the only posts for which native-born Turks were eligible were commissions in the feudal cavalry and regular cavalry, to which latter only the sons of slaves of Christian origin, or Turks in the first generation, were admitted. As another method of preventing the rise of an aristocracy of blood, measures were devised for putting to death the scions of the ruling dynasty or of leveling the descendents of royal princesses as quickly as possible into the masses. These were the well-known Law of Fratricide of Muhammad II, to which the numerous small coffins in the royal mausoleums bear tragic witness, and the Law of *Sanjaq* Bey of the same ruler, by which it was decreed that "the descendants of my daughters must not be appointed as *beylerbeys* [governors of provinces], but only as *sanjaq-beys* [governors of provincial districts]" or, in accord with a later extension of the law, as head gatekeepers (*qapuji-bashi*) and captains of galleys. In the reign of the young Ahmed I, the Law of Fratricide was commuted to imprisonment in the *Qafes* (literally "cage") in the royal harem, while, as a substitute measure for the Law of *Sanjaq* Bey, the sons of princesses were put out of the way at birth by the failure to tie the umbilical cord.

As evidence of the completeness with which the theory of government by a slave class was put into practice may be quoted the comment of the Venetian bailo Marcantonio Barbaro in 1584: "It is worthy of note that the wealth, the military power, and the government, in a word, the whole Ottoman state, is founded upon Moslem slaves born in the Christian faith." [7] Even more sweeping than this comment of the Venetian *bailo* is the report of Baron Wenceslas Wratislaw upon the occasion of his visit to Constantinople in 1591: "Never, therefore, did I hear it said of any pasha, or observe either in Constantinople or in the whole land of Turkey, that any pasha was a natural born Turk; on the contrary, kidnapped, or captured, or turned Turk." [8]

Slaves for the palace service were supplied through

capture, purchase, gift, and the Law of Tribute Children or the Law of Draft (*Devshirmeh*). Confronted with the problem of assimilating the hostile races of the Balkans and desirous, after a half century of continuous warfare, of releasing the population of Anatolia from conscription, Murad I, as has been said, established this famous law. Henceforth recruits for the army were drafted from the conquered European provinces, later including Albania, Bosnia, Bulgaria, Servia, Greece (with the exceptions only of the cities of Constantinople and Athens, Rhodes, and the Mainotes), from the Armenians who resided in these provinces, and from the Christian subjects of the Caucasus.[9] The law denied to the people of these countries the usual right accorded Christians of payment of the capitation tax in lieu of military service, and instead exacted as tribute a stipulated number of male children every three or four years. By the same law these youths were required to serve a novitiate of seven years in military schools provided for the purpose, or else in the royal palaces and upon royal domain, in the households of provincial governors and of high officials in the capital, or upon the cavalry fiefs of Anatolia.[10] In the sixteenth century the number of youths thus collected was from ten to twelve thousand once in three or four years, or an annual average of about three thousand, which in the seventeenth century fell to about two thousand. It is, however, to be especially noted that although the number of tribute youths constituted something less than one-half of the sum total of slaves recruited by every means for all the various departments of the royal service, the majority of the pages for the palace service were almost invariably selected from the tribute children. So long as the Law of Tribute Children was in force, therefore, it was the Christian youths of the Balkans who gave the tone and color to the Palace School and, in the end, to the Turkish government itself; Soqullu Muhammad Pasha, grand vizir under three sultans and probably the greatest of the holders of this office, was a tribute child from Croatia. It has even been asserted that "the advance of Islam and Turkish culture continued throughout the centuries, was notably through the application of the *Devshirmeh*." [11]

A second important source of supply for palace slaves, so long as the period of Turkish expansion lasted, was prisoners of war. As early as the reigns of Osman and Orkhan it had become the custom regularly to spare captives under the age of twenty. One-tenth of these became the property of the sultan and were usually attached to the palace service.[12] It was said that

merchants follow the sultan's army, also Janizaries and *Mangons* [Ordnance-operators?] mounted upon camels, who carry long iron chains, long enough to strangle, and to tie from fifty to sixty men of rank. These purchase from robbers and *procureurs* all those whom the sword of the enemy has pardoned. It is permitted them by law that they should render to the Prince one-tenth of the serfs and captives. The remainder they are permitted to keep and to sell as should seem good to them — a very common and fruitful traffic, no more and no less than the Romans in the past.[13]

On occasions during the full flush of conquest, when the number of the sultan's quota of prisoners of war was too large for the requirements of the royal service, as at the time of the conquest of the Balkans by Murad I, the surplus was sold in the public slave markets. Beginning with the reign of Murad III (1574–1595), the surplus was incorporated with the Janizary corps.[14] In proportion as the supply of prisoners of war decreased in the later period, the deficiency was supplied by means of the slave raids of the Crimean Tatars and Barbary Corsairs, tributary subjects of the Turkish sultans, whose methods and the tragic fate of whose victims are too well known to need recounting here. The Tatars were accustomed to gather frequently in bands of from two to three thousand at the city of Akeska, which was their most important meeting place, and thence to make incursions into those countries with which the Turks were constantly at war, into Russia, Poland, Bohemia, Hungary, and Austria, for the purpose of taking captive Christian youths. The choicest of these youths were sent to the sultan, the remainder being despatched to Zozerum to be sold in the slave market there.[15] Cicala Pasha, already spoken of in connection with his victory at the battle of Cerestes, is a striking example of a captive slave of "Frank" origin who was presented to Suleiman I and educated in the Palace School, and who afterwards became grand vizir.

Whenever the supply of tribute children, prisoners of war, and other captives proved inadequate, the deficiency was supplied by means of purchased slaves. This policy was not entirely a late one, for as early as the reign of Bayazid I the Turkish sultans had sought to improve the standard of their slaves by adding the choicest specimens to be found in the slave markets of the eastern Mediterranean and Black Sea coasts; when the usual sources of supply failed with the decline of the empire, it became the chief resource. These purchased slaves were chiefly from eastern Europe, Russia, Poland, Lithuania, and the subject population of the Caucasus. The Georgians and Circassians, whose physical types were especially admired by the Turks, found the slave trade with Constantinople so profitable that they maintained slave farms to meet the demand. They not only regularly captured children for the purpose of selling them in the Turkish slave markets, but even reared their own children with this end in view, considering the palace service the best possible opening for a brilliant career. Until the abolition of slavery by the Young Turks, the Circassians continued to form a large proportion of the Turkish slave population, especially of the harem slaves.

High Turkish officials, as well as the sultan, maintained large retinues of pages and educated them in household schools modeled after the pattern of the Palace School. Iskender Chelebi, treasurer under Suleiman the Magnificent, supported six thousand slaves in his household, six of whom rose to the position of vizir, and one, the famous Soqullu Muhammad already mentioned above, to that of grand vizir. The school for the pages of Soqullu Muhammad himself was famous for its size and for the excellent order maintained in it. Of the extent to which the custom of maintaining large numbers of pages had spread among Turkish officials in the latter half of the seventeenth century Rycaut writes:

I have observed, not only in the *Seraglio*, but also in the Courts of great men, their personal attendants have been of comely, lusty Youths, well habited, deporting themselves with singular Modesty and respect in the presence of their Master: so that when a *Pasha*, *Aga* (Chief), or *Spahee* travels, he is always attended with a comely equipage, followed by flourishing Youths, well clothed and mounted in great Numbers, that one may guess at the greatness of this Empire, by the retinue, pomp, and number of Servants which accompany Persons of Quality in their journeys; whereas in the parts of Christendom where I have travelled, I have observed (no not in attendance of Princes) such ostentation in Servants as is amongst the *Turks*, which is the life and Ornament of a Court.

It was the practice of these high officials to present slaves to the sultan in the hope that they might rise to important positions at court and reward their former owners with their patronage. By the time of Sultan Ibrahim (1640–1648), the gift of choice young slaves had come to be so greatly esteemed by the sultans that the purchase and education of slaves for the purpose of presentation to the sultans became "almost a speculation among Turkish officials." [16]

The sum total of slaves recruited from all these sources for all the various departments of the sultan's services numbered seven or eight thousand annually in the sixteenth century; in the seventeenth, the registers of the customhouse of Constantinople report the entry of about twenty thousand, including both sexes.[17] The number of pages in the Palace School of the Grand Seraglio during the reign of Muhammad II, as already given above, was three hundred and forty-odd.[18] During the reigns of Bayazid II and Selim I, the number in the Grand Seraglio is said to have been only three hundred, while in the two auxiliary schools of Adrianople and Galata *Saray* there were about three hundred each, or a sum total of about nine hundred in the three schools.[19] In the reign of Suleiman the Magnificent, who greatly increased the splendor of the royal state, the number of pages in the Grand Seraglio was more than double,[20] and the third and largest of the auxiliary schools, that of Ibrahim Pasha, was added. At the same time the number of royal pages was fixed by law at one thousand three hundred and fifty.[21] As a result of the extravagance which set in during the reign of Murad III and continued in progressive ratio for more than two centuries, the number of pages in the Grand Seraglio alone rose to eight or nine hundred — a figure which was maintained, with only occasional fluctuations, until the reforms of Selim III (1789–1808).[22] In 1585 Gian-francesco Morosini gives the incredibly large figure of six thousand in all four *sarays*,[23] and in the seventeenth century under the Kiuprulu vizirs there are said by Mehmed Khalifeh, himself a palace page, to have been "four thousand pages in the four schools who repeat the name of God and who pray for the sultan now and hereafter." [24] As a rule, however, after the suppression of the schools of Adrianople and of Ibrahim Pasha by Sultan Ibrahim, the total number of pages in the entire palace system does not appear to have exceeded two thousand. As a result of the reforming movement introduced by Mahmud II, the number of pages in the remaining schools of the Grand Seraglio and in the Galata *Saray* was reduced to six hundred.[25]

Whatever the origin of a slave, the same general requirements were observed for his admission either into the Palace School of the Grand Seraglio or into one of the auxiliary schools. In the fifteenth and sixteenth centuries the age of admission was usually from ten to fourteen years, although students were sometimes allowed to enter as young as eight years.[26] In the seventeenth century, when the slave system was no longer so rigidly enforced and the number of royal pages was at the same time greatly increased, pages of twenty years of age and more were sometimes admitted through the exercise of special influence.

Upon their arrival in Constantinople the tribute children, who had been collected by the palace gatekeepers, were brought before a board of expert examiners presided over by the chief white eunuch in his capacity as director-in-chief of the system of palace education, a procedure that was applied also to purchased slaves and prisoners of war. By a kind of test which in its shrewdness seems curiously to anticipate the modern intelligence test, and by an examination of physical points similar to those applied at a horse, dog, or cattle show, the youths were separated into two classes. The *sine qua non* of the sultan's service being physical beauty and bodily perfection, the most physically perfect, the most intelligent, and the most promising in every respect were set aside for the palace service; it is said that the Turks were unable to believe that a strong soul and a good mind could be found in a feeble or deformed body — a youth with a bodily defect, no matter how slight, was never admitted into the palace service.[27] The remainder, who were distinguished chiefly by reason of their physical strength and dexterity, were assigned to the Janizary corps. Those who had been set aside for the palace service were again separated into two classes. The comeliest and cleverest, "those, in whom, besides the accomplishment of the Body, they discover also a noble Genius, fit for a high Education, and such as may render them capable of Serving their Prince, sometime or other," were designated as student pages (*ich-oghlanlar*). The remainder, who were classified as novices or apprentices (*ajemi-oghlanlar*),[28] were put through a stiff course in manual training as gardeners or gatekeepers or halberdiers of the Grand Seraglio or other of the royal palaces, or less frequently, as artisans employed upon public works, preparatory to becoming members of the auxiliary corps, or irregulars, of the army.[29] From the group set apart for student pages, the cream was for a third time skimmed for the Palace School of the Grand Seraglio.[30] The remaining pages were then distributed among the three auxiliary schools, a certain proportion being reserved for the high officials of the capital and provinces who maintained schools for pages along lines similar to those of the palace schools.[31] When the process of examination and distribution had been duly completed, the pages were registered. The age, place of birth, name of parents, and new Turkish name of each page were entered in the school register (*ojaq defteri*), which was thereafter sent to the chancellery of the treasury for safekeeping.[32]

It was, as has been stated before, one of the chief policies of the Ottoman dynasty to inspire the devotion and loyalty of the governing class through close personal oversight and association with the pages of the Palace School. So important was this policy considered and so consciously was it pursued that even those sultans who, like Murad III, concerned themselves scarcely at all with the government made the Palace School one of

their chief preoccupations and even pastimes. They
took an especial interest in the selection of pages for
admission to the Grand Seraglio, particularly of those
who were admitted from one of the other palace
schools.[33] They frequently presided in person at the
examination, or inspection, of the pages at the time of
their admission, and always at the final ceremony on
their departure, which was made an impressive occasion. Menavino relates that, upon his arrival at the
Grand Seraglio in company with two other Italian boys,
all three were immediately conducted to the third court
and into the presence of Bayazid II. They were directed
to seat themselves — Menavino seating himself upon
the bottom step of a great marble staircase which faced
the west — and were then served with food, the sultan
meantime conversing with them through an interpreter
— in particular asking them questions about "our
Italy" — and being visibly amused with their efforts to
eat *a la Turca*. The repast finished, he tested their
ability to read and to write by directing them to write
and then to read aloud one another's writing. Menavino
was obliged to read to the sultan "stupid" things that
one of the other boys had written, but was rewarded
for his own accomplishments by the sultan's comment
"that Christians, especially Tuscans, are very clever,
because they are instructed from a very early age." [34]
The admission of Evliya Efendi, later the famous
traveler and author of *Narrative of Travels in Europe,
Asia and Africa in the Seventeenth Century*, directly to
the Hall of the Commissariat furnishes a still more
striking instance of the interest taken by the sultans in
the admission of students. It is, at the same time, an

example of the admission of freeborn Turks and other
Moslems in the later period of the Palace School. Having previously studied seven years in one of the *medresehs* of the capital, Evliya had already achieved signal
distinction as a student of the Koran; he also excelled
in music. In the hope of having him admitted to the
Palace School, his father, powerful as the chief of the
Goldsmiths' Guild of Constantinople, and his maternal
uncle, Melek Ahmed, at that time sword-bearer to the
Sultan and later grand vizir, conspired together to bring
their young relative to the attention of Murad IV
(1623–1640). They contrived that, on the great festival
of the Night of Power, Evliya should be one of the
muezzins (those who make the five daily calls to prayer)
in Santa Sophia, which mosque it was the custom for the
sultans to attend upon that occasion. What occurred
is best described in Evliya's own words:

After the prayer *Teravih*, I began to repeat from memory
nearly the whole of the Koran. When I had finished the
Sura Ena'am, Guzbegji [custodian of the harem] Mohammed
Agha and the *Salihdar* [sword bearer] Melek Ahmed, came
up to the seat, and putting on my head, in the presence of
thousands, a turban wrought with gold, informed me that
the emperor desired to see me. They then took me by the
hand and led me into the *mahfil* [royal box] of the emperor.
On beholding the dignified countenance of Sultan Murad,
I bowed and kissed the ground. The emperor received me
very graciously, and after the salutations, asked me in how
many hours I could repeat the Koran. I said, if it please God,
if I proceed at a quick rate I can repeat it in seven hours, but
if I do it moderately, without much variation of the voice, I
can accomplish it in eight hours. The sultan then said,
"Please God! he may be admitted into the number of my
intimate associates in the room of the deceased Musa." He

then gave me two or three handfuls of gold, which altogether amounted to 623 pieces. Though I was then only a youth of twenty-five, I was sufficiently well educated, and my manners were polished, having been accustomed to associate with viziers and muftis, in whose presence I had more than once repeated the As'har and Na't of the sacred volume. Murad left the mosque in the usual style with flambeaux and lanterns. I mounted a horse, and entered the imperial serai by the cypress gate. The emperor next repaired to the Khasoda, and recommending me to the Chief, directed him to invest me with the *kaftan* [robe of honor], in the chamber of the Kilarji bashi [Chief of the Commissariat]. He then retired to the inner harem. Next morning he surrendered me to the Kilarji bashi Safid Agha, and a room was assigned me in the apartments of the Kilar [Commissariat].

With his own hand the sultan wrote an order to the Head Treasurer for Evliya's textbooks. He also honored him by presenting him with a Koran, a silver inkstand set with jewels, a writing-board inlaid with pearls, a tambourine studded with jewels, a fur robe, and a sable *qalpaq* (hat).[35]

Following the policy inaugurated by Muhammad II, the sultans kept personal oversight of the progress and well-being of the pages of the Grand Seraglio by going constantly among them while they were studying and even, as has been said, by occasional rounds of the halls in disguise at night. It was one of their favorite pastimes to watch the school games and practice of physical exercises. The three auxiliary schools they also inspected in person from time to time. They were accustomed to pass part of the night which precedes the festival of *Buyuk Bayram*, or Great Bayram, in the Hall of the Royal Bedchamber. On the eve of *Sheker Bayram*, or Bayram of Sweets, it was their custom to repair to the

Great Hall, which was the general assembly hall of the
school, and there to listen to the discourse of the pages
upon philosophy and morals, and to review their sports
— to hold what was in reality a kind of annual general
examination. Above all else they made a point of recog-
nizing merit by a system of rewards and of bestowing
these rewards in person, in particular for excellence in
the Arabic language and in penmanship. These rewards were usually in the form of money, or robes of
cloth of gold and silver and of brocade, sometimes even
of a banquet tendered an individual student. Hafiz
Elias Bey records in his journal upon the fifteenth day
of the month of Ramazan, 1243 A.H. (1828), on which
day it was the custom of the sultans to scatter coins of
gold and silver to the palace pages, that Mahmud II
ordered the sword-bearer to have the money brought to
the palace and that in addition the grand vizir and three
high officers of the army sent fifty thousand piastres for
the same purpose. It was reckoned at this time that
each page received as his share the sum of two hundred
and fifty-five piastres.[36]

The general administration and surveillance of the
palace schools was in charge of the white eunuchs, who
in their relation to the school were designated as
muzakerejiler, literally trainers or drill masters; the
teaching staff, as has already been said, were as a rule
nonresident. As the practice of castration was forbidden by Moslem law, all eunuchs were imported,
white eunuchs generally from the Caucasus region and,
in the seventeenth century, also from certain states of
India. The average cost in the slave market of a white
eunuch, who as a class were only partially castrated,

was from one hundred to one hundred and fifty crowns, or about one-fourth the cost of a completely castrated black eunuch, for whom the price demanded usually ranged from four hundred to six hundred crowns. Although the duties of the white eunuchs of the Grand Seraglio, who were also chamberlains of the Outer Palace and guardians of the Imperial Gate and later of the Gate of Felicity, were much more extensive than those of the black eunuchs, the relative value of the two at the time of purchase continued to hold in their wages. The chief white eunuch received one hundred sequins a day, while the chief black eunuch received three hundred. Exclusive of the commissioned officers, the average daily wage of a white eunuch in the sixteenth and seventeenth centuries was from twelve to fifteen *aqchas*, with keep and emoluments of office,[37] while that of a black eunuch for the same period was from twenty to twenty-five *aqchas*, with unlimited opportunity in addition for amassing riches by means of gifts from the sultan and the women of the royal harem.

Selected for admission to the palace at about the same age as the pages, the white eunuchs received precisely the same education as the pages, those in the Grand Seraglio usually completing the entire course, including service in the Hall of the Royal Bedchamber.[38] During the reign of Muhammad II the number of white eunuchs employed in the Grand Seraglio was twenty-three, and the entire number in the royal employ some forty-odd.[39] After the introduction of black eunuchs as guards of the royal harem and the consequent restriction of the white eunuchs to the service of the royal *selamlik*, the number of the latter employed in the Grand Seraglio was usually in the ratio of one to about ten pages. There were eighty during the early part of the sixteenth century,[40] and one hundred and twenty during the first half of the reign of Muhammad IV (1648–1687).[41] As the result of enforced retrenchments in palace expenditure, in the second half of the same reign the number was reduced to fifty.[42] With the extravagant sultans of the eighteenth century it was again increased to one hundred or more.[43] With the reforms of Selim III and Mahmud II, and the consequent decline in the importance of the school, the number fell to thirty or forty.[44]

The organization of the white eunuchs constituted a rigid and elaborate hierarchy. The chief white eunuch, who was head gatekeeper of the Grand Seraglio, head of the Inner Service, grand master of ceremony, and confidential agent of the sultan, was also the director-in-chief of the system of palace schools. For a century and a half his was the most important post at the Turkish court and in consequence one of great political influence.[45] A typical day's program illustrates the nature of his duties in relation to the Palace School. At five o'clock in the morning he received the heads of the various halls in his apartment, after which he made the rounds of the entire school and gave the orders for the day. He then waited upon the sultan and, after being summoned, upon the queen-mother, for the purpose of receiving their orders for the day. The interval between the conclusion of these visits and the midday meal was reserved for attendance at court, in the event of the reception of ambassadors, provincial governors, or other officials. He was then served his repast in his own apartment, the only official of the Inner Service so

privileged, and afterwards enjoyed the additional privilege of a well-earned siesta. In the late afternoon he
received the pages in his apartment, and upon the ter-
mination of these visits, made a second round of the
school halls.[46]

Following the chief white eunuch in order of rank in
the hierarchy of white eunuchs in the fifteenth and sixteenth centuries were the head treasurer, the head commissary, the palace steward (saray aghasi), and the
first officer of the Hall of the Royal Bedchamber.[47]
Dating from the degradation of the head treasurer by
Murad IV, the order of rank of these officers was shifted
as follows: the first officer of the Royal Bedchamber,
the palace steward, the head treasurer, and the head
commissary.[48] The first officer of the Royal Bedchamber, who was also first chamberlain of the palace and
keeper of one of the three imperial seals, was in charge
of the discipline of the Palace School. The head
treasurer and the head commissary, the latter also general superintendent of the kitchens and head butler of
the sultan,[49] were the nominal heads of the halls of pages
attached to their departments. Eunuchs without titles
were classified as noncommissioned officers (neferler).[50]

In view of the heavy duties of the chief white eunuch
in connection with the court, the greater part of the administrative routine of the Palace School was delegated
to the palace steward. This official, whose primary
duty in the Grand Seraglio was that of superintendent
of buildings, and who, in the absence of both the sultan
and chief white eunuch, acted as chatelain of the
palace, held the post of assistant director of the Palace
School. He was also head, or supervisor, of three of the

halls, the Hall of the Expeditionary Force, the Great
Hall, and the Small Hall,[51] and paymaster and quartermaster of the inner service. In the capacity of assistant
director of the school, he, too, made a daily report to
the sultan. In actual fact, so largely did the practical
administration of the Palace School devolve upon him
that in his relation to the school he was known as *ustad*,
or "master," and also as *murebbi*, or "he who trains." [52]

Ranking next to these officers of the general administration, there was attached to each of the halls an *oda
bashi*, or first officer, who, under the Code of Laws of
Muhammad II, was responsible for the order and discipline of his hall; he usually slept there, and in person
inspected the coffers of the pages in order to see that
they contained no sweets, spices, or love letters.[53]
There was also a second officer in each hall known as
the steward (*ketkhuda* or *kihayeh*).[54] Each hall had its
own librarian, who had charge of the common textbooks; its recorder, who each day called the roll and
recorded the marks of the students; and its treasurer,
who received the allowance for each student of that
hall, deposited it in a separate bag, and delivered the
bag to the owner only when he left the palace. To each
hall was also assigned one imam, or leader of ritual, and
three muezzins. In addition to these officers, there
were also student officers, the number of which varied
according to rank and size of the hall, the Hall of the
Royal Bedchamber and the Great Hall being the most
heavily staffed. There were twelve student officers each
in the halls of the Expeditionary Force, Commissariat,
and Treasury, appointed in order of seniority.[55]

The pages of each hall were divided into companies

of ten, the members of each company addressing each other by the pet name of *lala dash* — literally, "companion under the same male nurse." Within these same companies the older pages had younger pages assigned to them, whom they assisted with their studies and in the care of their clothing. Over each company was a *lala* (male nurse)[56] or *qadi-oghlan* (pedagogue) whose duty it was to keep order among the pages of his company in the classroom, to preside over them during meals, and to sleep next them at night. At a late date these *lalas* were to some extent recruited from the student body. When a page had attained the age of thirty and at the same time displayed marked proficiency in his studies, he was frequently given the title of *lala*, and permitted to assist the surveillance officers by the recording of marks, and to help the younger pages with their studies.[57] An entry in the journal of Hafiz Elias Bey records that at the time of the reorganization of the Turkish army by Mahmud II, as the result of which thirty pages were transferred from Galata *Saray* to the halls of the Treasury, Commissariat, and Expeditionary Force, to be drilled according to the new methods, "each page was put under the care of a *lala*." [58] In cases of unusual ability, a *lala* might even be promoted to the rank of *qalfa* or *khalifa*, an under-master, who taught the Koran.[59]

The teaching staff of the palace schools, as has been said before, was in the main composed of members of the Ulema, although it frequently included also some of the most famous lay scholars, mathematicians, musicians, and poets of the day.[60] Instruction was given by means of daily classes and by periodic lectures designed

for the entire student body. At the beginning of the
sixteenth century there were four masters (*khalifeh*) who
taught Turkish, Arabic, Persian, and the Koran to the
pages of the Great Hall,[61] and in the seventeenth century, seven. In the second half of the same century,
there were twelve masters each in the halls of the
Treasury, Commissariat, and Expeditionary Force.[62]
As a rule the general lectures were given either by members of the Ulema who held a rank not lower than that
of professor (*muderris*), or else by scholars (*danish-
mendler*) who had attained distinction in some particular field. In 1612, when the total number of students in
the five halls was eight or nine hundred, forty scholars
went daily from the city to the Grand Seraglio,[63] those
who taught the most advanced classes going to the
palace only once a week, usually Tuesdays. In the third
quarter of the seventeenth century there were nine
general lectures a week in the school of the Grand
Seraglio; of this number Evliya Muhammad Efendi, a
former tutor of the noted traveler of the same name,
specialist in the Koran, and at the time imperial imam,
gave two. On Wednesday and Saturday of each week
some eminent calligrapher gave demonstrations of his
art before the entire student body.[64] All members of
the teaching staff were accorded signal distinction
within the palace precincts. Upon the arrival of a member of the staff at the *Bab-i Humayun* he was received
by a waiting attendant (*khoja hizmetkiarlari*), who
escorted him with ceremony to his accustomed place.
Upon his arrival in a hall the pages kissed his hand, a
mark of deference which was introduced into the Palace
School at the time of Muhammad II and made a law by

Bayazid II. Nonresident teachers were accorded the privilege of the common room in the third court, and they were served their meals in the Small Hall with the officers of that chamber.[65] But in the matter of financial compensation the teaching staff of the Palace School fared as badly as do the members of the academic profession today. The regular stipend varied from eight to twelve *aqchas* a day, with accouterments, which sum was little more than one-half of the wage of a white eunuch and no more than the allowance of a page of the Imperial Treasury.[66] For unusual excellence on the part of his students the sultans sometimes bestowed a robe of honor and a fur *qaftan* upon the instructor, and students at graduation were accustomed to present their teachers with a purse of five hundred *aqchas*.[67] Apparently the teaching staff of the Palace School must have found their reward in the recognized quality of the work done and the dignity accorded them, rather than in monetary compensation.

CHAPTER IV

THE CURRICULUM

THE type of governing official which the Turkish sultans desired to produce through the medium of their palace system of education was the warrior-statesman and loyal Moslem who, at the same time, should be "a man of letters and a gentleman of polished speech, profound courtesy, and honest morals." [1] To this end a student of the Palace School, from the day of his admission until he quitted the Grand Seraglio, was meticulously drilled in the ceremonies of the Moslem religion and Turkish etiquette. A contemporary judgment bears witness to the effectiveness of this social training: "The Turkish nobles, pages, people of the court and palace are reared in a politeness which excels the politeness and urbanity of other nations." [2] The pages received instruction also, in almost equal proportions, in the liberal arts, in the art of war and physical exercise, and in vocational training — a combination which seems to have been paralleled only by the samurai, the warrior-scholars of Japan.[3] The liberal arts, in the Turkish, or Islamic, interpretation of the term, embraced the Turkish, Arabic, and Persian languages; Turkish and Persian literatures; Arabic grammar and syntax; a study of the Koran and leading commentaries upon it; Moslem theology, jurisprudence, and law; and Turkish history, music, and mathematics. Of the last subject the only branch which is known with certainty to have been taught in the palace schools is arithmetic,[4] although it seems likely that instruction may also have been given in geometry. The great Turkish architect of the sixteenth century, Sinan Bey, who was educated in one of the Janizary barracks in Constantinople, probably that in the Hippodrome, almost certainly received some instruction in geometry as preparation for his later work as an engineer, and it is a well-established fact that the curriculum of the Palace School was much more comprehensive and advanced than that provided for the Janizaries. Rycaut, writing in 1668, maintains that as for

Other Sciences, as Logick, Physick, Metaphysick, Mathematicks, and other our University Learning, they [the Turks] are wholly ignorant; unless in the latter, as far as Musick is a part of Mathematicks, whereof there is a school apart in the *Seraglio*. Only some that live in *Constantinople* have learned some certain rules of Astrology, which they exercise upon all occasions, and busie themselves in Prophesies of future contingences of the Affairs of the Empire, and the unconstant estate of great Ministers, in which their predictions seldom divine grateful or pleasing stories. Neither have the wisest and most active Ministers or Souldiers amongst them, the least inspection into Geography, whereby to be acquainted with the situation of Countreys or disposition of the Globe, though they themselves enjoy the possession of so large a portion of the Universe. Their Sea-men, who seldom venture beyond sight of Land (unless they be those of *Barbary*, who are *Renegadoes* and practised in the Christian Arts of Navigation) have certain *Sea-carts* ill-framed, and the Capes and headlands so ill laid down, that in their Voyages from *Constantinople* to *Alexandria*, the richest place of their Trade, they trust more to their eye and experience, then the direction of their Maps; nor could I ever see any Cart of the black Sea made either by *Turk* or *Greek* which could give the least light to a knowing Seaman, so as to encourage him according to the rules of Art, to lay any confidence thereon in his Navigation.[5]

On the other hand, the Abbate Toderini, writing in 1787, when learning had already suffered a decline, says that

the Turks of Constantinople are very versed in the science of numbers; indeed they are so well instructed in this respect that they astonish European mathematicians. The libraries of Constantinople are filled with books on arithmetic in both Turkish and Arabic. Of algebra, which they use in connection with astrology and divination, treatises are to be found in occasional libraries, and there are also certain young Turks, especially the students of the Valideh Mosque, who employ European textbooks on the subject. The Turks study geometry for the sake of astronomy, navigation, maps and calendars, to which they are devoted. The best edition of Euclid available to them is the Arabic translation of Nassiredn Al-Thussi, a publication of the de Medici Press in 996 A.H. (1557/8).[6]

This evidence of Toderini is supported by von Hammer, who says that the Turks were not without interest in and knowledge of geography, as shown "by the prowess of such noted seamen as Piale, Torghoud, Salih, who reigned in the Aegean and Mediterranean Seas, and as Piri-Reis, Murad, and Sidi-Ali in the Gulfs of Arabia and Persia," who, "while establishing other claims to fame, at the same time augmented the knowledge of their nation by their geographies and nautical works." [7]

Physical training was begun with gymnastic exercises, and from these progressed to sports of various kinds, cavalry exercises, and other "arts of war." As a result of the systematic and long-continued training which they received, the students of the Palace School are said to have developed amazing strength and agility of body, vigorous health, and unusual skill in arms; to an extraordinary degree they were rendered "fit for the Wars and all active employments." [8] The high standard of physical development which they attained may be judged from the fact that there was no finer army in Europe than the Turkish army during the centuries when the palace system of education was at the height of its efficiency, and that practically all the officers of the regular cavalry, or cavalry of the Sublime Porte, and many of the officers of the feudal cavalry, had been trained in the Palace School.

In the Traditions the Prophet Muhammad is reported to have said that "he who earns is a dearly beloved friend of Allah" (*Al-Kasib habibu-llah*). Perhaps as a result of this teaching — and perhaps not less as a provision against the inconstancy of fate in an oriental despotism — all Turks, with the exception of the Janizaries,[9] no matter how high their stations, were formerly accustomed to learn "some art and occupation according to the capacity of their spirit." [10] In view of the early contact of the Turks with the Chinese, there is interest in Dr. Hu Shih's statement that even today "a Chinese student must learn some useful art." [11] Concerning the wide prevalence of this custom among the Turks, Theodoros Spandouginos wrote in 1519, "There is not any prince or lord so great, even the Emperor himself, that he does not cause his children to be instructed in some art or science, by means of which he could earn a livelihood in case he should fall upon evil days." [12] Some of the sultans excelled in their chosen crafts. Muhammad II, who took an interest in gardens unusual even for a Turk, was himself a skilled gardener, as has already been said, and often worked with the spade, rake, and other tools in the gardens of the Grand Seraglio [13] or other royal palaces: "this same Muhammad was also accustomed to fashion rings for the bow, buckles for the girdle and sheaths for the sword, which things he did merely for passing the time." [14] His grandson and great-grandson, Selim I and Suleiman I, were both skilled goldsmiths; [15] Selim II produced in large quantities the crescents which pilgrims were accustomed to mount upon the staffs which they carried to the Holy Cities; Murad III manufactured arrows, and Ahmed I the type of ivory ring which archers wore upon their thumbs, upon which he is said to have labored assiduously; [16] and so on down to Abd ul-Hamid II, several specimens of whose fine Damascene inlaid work may be seen in the Mejidiyeh Kiushk. The arts and crafts which were taught the pages in the four schools of vocational training of the Grand Seraglio were in each case determined by the lines of the palace service to which these schools were attached, or else by the specific services which a page performed for the sultan.

But above all it was the aim of the Turkish sultans to discover and to train youths of exceptional ability for leadership in the state. Of the unusual degree to which individual aptitude or talent was appreciated by the Turks, Ogier Ghiselin de Busbecq, ambassador from the Holy Roman Empire to the Sublime Porte during the reign of Suleiman the Magnificent and author of one of the most vivid and searching records of that remarkable reign, writes:

The Turks rejoice greatly when they find an exceptional man as though they had acquired a precious object, and they spare no labor or effort in cultivating him; especially if they discern that he is fit for war. Our plan [that is, in Western Europe] is very different; for if we find a good dog, hawk, or horse, we are greatly delighted, and we spare nothing to bring it to the greatest perfection of its kind. But if a man happens to possess an extraordinary disposition, we do not take like pains; nor do we think that his education is especially our affair; and we receive much pleasure and many kinds of service from the well-trained horse, dog, and hawk; but the Turks much more from a well-educated man (*ex homine bonis moribus informato*) in proportion as the nature of a man is more admirable and more excellent than that of the other animals.[17]

The chief means employed to stimulate students to the maximum of effort were a large measure of freedom in the choice of subjects of study, and a system of merit consisting of carefully graded rewards and corresponding punishments. In the third quarter of the seventeenth century, Jean-Claude Flachat observed that "the dispositions and inclinations of the pages were carefully consulted." [18] The course of study within broad lines was almost entirely a matter of choice, the only absolutely prescribed subjects being the Turkish and Arabic languages and the Koran. In addition to the prescription of these two subjects there existed only the one general requirement that a page "should work at something and should work in earnest, drones only not being permitted." In actual fact the pages are said to have devoted day and night to the study of the "sciences," using their recreation time for required physical or manual exercises, or for study.[19] To quote again from Flachat: "The pages apply themselves very seriously to study. They make it their duty to excel, as that is the only means which they have of attaining success. This ambition gives rise among them to a praiseworthy emulation." [20]

The system of merit of the Palace School, which was a replica of the carefully graded rewards of merit underlying the hierarchy of the government, prevailed in the school from its first foundation until the final breaking up of the ancient system of slave government. Promotions from one hall to another, appointments to student offices and later to military and administrative positions, all were based strictly upon the merit system. Busbecq asserts that the workings of this system in the government were paralleled by its workings in the palace system of education:

No distinction is attached to birth among the Turks; the deference to be paid a man is measured by the position he holds in the public service. There is no fighting for precedence; a man's place is marked out by the duties he discharges. In making his appointments the Sultan pays no regard to any pretensions on the score of wealth or rank, nor does he take into consideration recommendations or popularity; he considers each case on its own merits, and examines carefully into the character, ability, and disposition of the man whose promotion is in question. It is by merit that men rise in the service, a system which ensures that posts should be assigned only to the competent. Each man in Turkey carries in his own hand his ancestry and his position in life, which he may make or mar as he will. Those who receive the highest offices from the Sultan are for the most part the sons of shepherds or herdsmen, and so far as being ashamed of their parentage, they actually glory in it, and consider it a matter of boasting that they owe nothing to the accident of birth; for they do not believe that high qualities are either natural or hereditary, nor do they think that they can be handed down from father to son, but that they are partly the gift of God, and partly the result of good training, great industry, and unwearied zeal; arguing that high qualities do not descend from a father to his son or heir, any more than a talent for music, mathematics, or the like; and that the mind does not derive its origin from the father, so that the son should necessarily be like the father in character, but emanates from heaven, and is thence infused into the human body. Among the Turks, therefore, honours, high posts, and judgeships are the rewards of great ability and good service. If a man be dishonest, or lazy, or careless, he remains at the bottom of the ladder, an object of contempt; for such qualities there are no honours in Turkey! [21]

An additional incentive to merit was provided by scholarships, or allowances, on a differential scale according to rank, for the six halls of the Grand Seraglio and the three affiliated schools as shown in the accompanying table. There was ample precedent for these student scholarships in the early *medresehs* of Nizam ul-Mulk and others. It is also not unlikely that Muhammad may have known of the "peculiar fancy" of Sultan Firuz Tughlaq "for educating slaves, of whom there were altogether eighteen thousand for whose maintenance and comfort he took special care. . . . He made suitable provision for the bestowal of stipends and scholarships upon the successful students, and over and above these, every inmate of the *madrasah*, be he a student, professor, or traveller lodging there, received a fixed daily allowance for his maintenance." [22]

Punishments for failure in the performance of duty or for infringement of regulations were frequent and severe but at the same time were kept within distinct limits.

Date	Great Hall	Small Hall	Hall of Expeditionary Force	Hall of Commissariat	Hall of Treasury
Ca. 1470–1481 (Angiolello)	. . .	. . .	. . .	. . .	. . .
Ca. 1502 (Menavino) . . . . First year: 2 Second year: 3 Third year: 2		. . .	. . .	7	10–15
1537 (Junis Bey)	. . .	. . .	. . .	. . .	. . .
1542 (Antoine Geuffroy)	. . .	. . .	. . .	. . .	. . .
1560 (Postel)	. . .	. . .	. . .	. . .	. . .
Reign of Suleiman I (von Hammer, *Histoire*, X, 196)	8	8	. . .	8	10
1612 (Vigenère)	7–8	10–12	12	8–10	10–15
1660 (Hezarfen Husein Efendi) . .	10	10	10	10	12
1665 (Bobovi)	8	8	12	12	12
1668 (Rycaut, *Present State*)	4–5	4–5	8	. . .	. . .
1684 (Pétis de La Croix, *Mémoires*)	8	8	10	10	12

* Rate of allowance is in *aqchas per diem*, except where otherwise stated. Fifty aqchas had the value of one Venetian gold ducat.

Hall of Royal Bedchamber (exclusive of officers)	Average rate of allowance in Grand Seraglio	Sum total of appropriations for pages of Grand Seraglio	Average rate in Adrianople Saray	Average rate in Galata and Ibrahim Pasha Sarays	Sum total of appropriations for Galata and Ibrahim Pasha Sarays
20	8	. . .	. . .	. . .	. . .
6–7 ducats per month)	. . .	. . .	. . .	. . .	. . .
. . .	. . .	10,000	. . .	. . .	. . .
18–20	6–7	. . .	. . .	. . .	. . .
. . .	10–14	2,500	12	6–10 (Galata Saray)	. . .
25	. . .	. . .	. . .	. . .	. . .
10–15	. . .	. . .	. . .	. . .	. . .
30	. . .	6,400,000 (per annum)	. . .	. . .	6,626,392 (per annum)
40	. . .	. . .	. . .	. . .	. . .
. . .	. . .	. . .	. . .	. . .	. . .
. . .	. . .	10,600 (270 purses, keysehs)	. . .	. . .	. . .

Penalties for ordinary offenses were scolding, fasting, deprivation of the more popular physical exercises, especially boxing, running, and leaping, and also flogging with a long slender lash or stick on the soles of the feet, in an ordinary offense to the number of ten strokes (*falaqa*). It was expressly forbidden that either officers of the school or outside teachers should administer corporal punishment more than once in one day to the same pupil; anyone who exceeded this limit was dismissed from the school, or, if the offense were flagrant, suffered the loss of one of his hands.[23]

Without question the training of the Palace School during its best period was arduous — austere and relentless. It was the opinion of Rycaut that

he who hath run through the several Schools, Orders and degrees of the *Seraglio*, must needs be an extraordinary mortified man, patient of all labours, services, and injunctions, which are imposed on him with a strictness beyond the discipline that religious novices are acquainted with in Monastries, or the severity of *Capuchins*, or holy Votaries. But yet methinks these men that have been used all their lives to servitude, and subjection, should have their spirit abased, and when licensed from the *Seraglio* to places of Trust and Government, should be so acquainted how to obey, as to be ignorant how to Rule, and be dazzled with the light of liberty, and overjoyed with the sence of their present condition, and past sufferings, passing from one extream to another, that they should lose their reasons, and forget themselves and others. But in answer hereunto, the *Turks* affirm, that none know so well how to govern, as those who have learned how to obey; though at first the sence of their freedom may distract them, yet afterwards the discipline, lectures, and morality in their younger years, will begin to operate, and recollect their scattered sences into their due and natural places.[24]

The military decline of the seventeenth and eighteenth centuries and the consequent change in national policy, especially the increased importance of diplomacy rather than arms as a weapon of defense, made itself felt less in the courses of study of the Palace School than in its code of behavior. The ideal page as described at the beginning of the nineteenth century reflects the fundamental change which had taken place in the methods of government:

A page must keep silent as the woodcutter Andreas in a Russian peasant's house, and comport himself in general as if honey were on his tongue and oil of almonds on his back. At times he must be blinder than a mole, deafer than a heathcock, more insensible than a polypus; but again at other times he must have the eyes of a lynx and the ear of a Pomeranian wolf-dog. He must learn to turn his eyes always upon the ground and to keep his arms always crossed over his breast. In proportion as he approaches manhood he must become more circumspect, inclined to make friends of all whom he meets and enemies of none, for even the meanest may often defeat one's ends. He must trust no one, but always suspect the worst, though feigning the contrary. . . . Mankind is as a rule wicked; self-interest is the mainspring of action, and virtue is mere hypocrisy.[25]

In spite of the transformation in ideal the curriculum seems to have suffered little outward, or formal, change during the three centuries and a half that the Palace School remained the military and political school of the Ottoman state. Instruction in the liberal arts was begun in the preparatory period and continued throughout the course. Particular stress was put upon the study of the Turkish language, which students of the palace schools were required to speak, read, and write fluently and correctly — no small undertaking, even for a Turk. Three lists of the books in use in the school in the seventeenth century, which offer valuable evidence concerning the curriculum,[26] include no Turkish grammars or books of syntax, which, it was said, "were entirely lacking among the Turks. They say that they have no need of them and that they learn enough by usage and habit of speaking. . . . There are some Turkish grammars, but all are made by the French and are used only by them." [27] Turkish books which are included in the lists belong chiefly to a genre known as *Mulamma*, narrative romances, or collections of short tales, characterized by a very ornate style with an unusually large admixture of Arabic and Persian words. It was a very popular form of literature with "the most airy and ingenious spirits" among the palace pages, and it is suggested that "the great difference between the speech of those who were educated in the Saray and of those educated outside, which was derived from the books which they read," probably resulted from the reading of this type of romance.[28] Several of the most popular were a translation of the *Arabian Nights* into Turkish; the *Sayyid Battal* or *Battal Ghazi*, an epic of the struggle of an Arab hero against paganism in behalf of Islam, a story which enjoyed a perennial popularity among Turkish soldiers and Arab peasants; the *History of Forty Vizirs* (*Qirq Wazir*), a compilation in prose of Turkish folk tales of different periods; and the *Story of Kalila wa-Dimna* or the *Royal Book* (*Humayun Nameh*), a book of fables translated from Indian into Pahlevi, thence into Arabic, and from Arabic into Turkish in the reign of Murad III. All of these romances are still in

circulation today, a remarkable testimony to the degree
to which they were representative of the national spirit
and ideals and to the wisdom of their selection. Twelve
different styles of calligraphy were taught in the Palace
School.[29] Students who specialized in calligraphy usually aspired to secretarial positions in some one of the
various lines of government service, or to the higher
offices of government. Rycaut, who was one of the
first to make a study of the Turkish polity, says of the
calligraphers: "Those others who are of a complexion
more melancholick and inclinable to contemplation,
proceed with more patience of method, and are more
exact in their studies, intending to become Masters of
their Pen, and by that means to arrive to honour and
office either of Rest [*Reis*] Efendi, or Secretary of State,
Lord Treasurer, or Secretary of the Treasury, or Dispensatory." The same authority bears witness to the
study of Turkish history and law as follows: "Yet as
to the successes and progress of Affairs in their own
Dominions, they [the pages] keep most strict Registers
and Records, which serve them as Presidents [*sic*] and
Rules for the present Government of their Affairs." [30]
It was in the Palace School that the majority of the
official chroniclers were trained — the so-called palace
historians (*saray vaqaa-nuvisi*), inaugurated by Muhammad II and continued by his successors in almost un-
broken sequence down to Abd ur-Rahman Sherif Efendi
in the present generation.

The Arabic and Persian languages and literatures
have been well styled "the humanities of Islamic culture." At the height of the influence of the Palace
School a knowledge of Arabic as the key to the Koran

and other authoritative sources of the Holy Law (*Shariah*) was esteemed a "necessary accomplishment of a *Pasha*, or any great Minister in relation to the better discharge of his office, being thereby enabled to have an inspection into the writings and sentences of the *Kadees* (*Qadis*), or other officers of the Law within his jurisdiction, as well as furnished with knowledge and matter of discourse concerning religion." [31] From the first day of their matriculation students were taught the prescribed manner of saying the five daily prayers and of reciting the Koran. During the course of one year they were drilled in the intricacies of the Arabic alphabet and thoroughly instructed in the principles of the grammar and syntax.

The Arabic grammars which were in use when Bobovi was a page in the Palace School were *Kitab al-bina*, *Kitab al-Maqsud*, *Kitab al-Izzi*,[32] and also *Marah al-arwah*.[33] These deal with accidence. The textbooks dealing with syntax were: the *Misbah* of al-Mutarrizi, the *Ajurrumiya* of Ibn Ajurrumi, the *Kafiya* of Ibn al-Hajib with its commentary by the Persian poet Jami.[34] Their Arabic dictionaries were the *Lughat Akhtari* of Muslih al-Din Mustafa al-Qarahisari [35] and *Subha-i sibyan* (*The Rosary of Children*), of which a manuscript dated as late as A.H. 1256 (1840/1) exists in one of the Suleimaniya *medresehs*.

When a sufficient acquaintance with the Arabic language had been acquired, the student began the study of commentaries on the Koran and of traditions and treatises on Muslim jurisprudence, theology, and law. The chief commentary on the Koran was that of al-Baidawi (*Enwar al-Tanzil*), commonly called *Tefsir-i*

Qadi, while the collections of Traditions studied included the *Sahih* of al-Bukhari, the *Sunan* of Ibn Majah, and the *Sahih* of Muslim. Among the treatises on theology and law those in most common use were the *Shurat al-salat* and the *Sharia* of Sadr al-Sharia,[36] the *Multaqa al-abhur* of Ibrahim al-Halabi,[37] the *Muqaddima* of Ahmad b. Muhammad al-Shaznawi,[38] the *Mukhtasar* of Ahmad b. Muhammad al-Quduri,[39] and the *Hidaya* of Burhan ad-Din Ali al-Marghinani.[40] A student of the Palace School who specialized in the study of the Holy Law usually aspired to become an imam in one of the royal mosques, a position which insured a competency and was a life sinecure; a palace *juzkhan*, one who can recite a part of the Koran for the repose of the soul of someone who had made legal provision for that purpose; or a *hafiz*, a professional reciter of the Koran, who can recite the entire book from memory. Those students who specialized in the edicts of the sultans and other ordinances of civil law aimed at some charge of judicature.[41]

The Persian language was the courtly language of the nearer Orient and the key to the literature of chivalry and romance. Rycaut summarizes the reasons for its study by the students of the Palace School as follows:

It fits them with quaint words and eloquence, becoming the Court of their Prince, and corrects the grossness, and enriches the barrenness of the *Turkish* tongue, which in itself is void both of expression and sweetness of accent. It teaches them also a handsome and gentle deportment, instructs them in Romances, raises their thoughts to aspire to the generous and virtuous actions they read of in the *Persian* Novellaries, and endues them with a kind of *Platonick* love to each other, which is accompanied with a true friendship amongst some few, and with as much gallantry as is exercised in any part of the world.[42]

Students of the Palace School were promoted to the study of Persian as soon as they had attained proficiency in Turkish and Arabic. No mention is made of the use of Persian grammars. The dictionary employed was that of Shahdi,[43] which is written partly in prose and partly in verse. The books most commonly read were the *Book of Advice* (*Pend-Nama*) by Ferid ad-Din Attar, the *Gulistan* and the *Bostan* of Saadi, and a fourth book with the title of *Danisten*, which may be the *Danishnama-yi Alayi* of Avicenna.[44] As exercises in composition students wrote poetry and translated books, with commentaries appended, in both Arabic and Persian.[45] Students who specialized in Persian usually had in view positions either as secretaries or as chancellors.[46]

In addition to the textbooks already mentioned, the pages had at their disposal the resources of the Library of Ahmed III, which, as has already been said in Chapter II above, stood in the center of the quadrangle of the Palace School. The historian Rashid Efendi says of the history of the books in this library:

There was a multitude of choice and precious books in the Royal Treasury of the Saray, in part gifts to the government and in part acquired by the government from the beginning of the Ottoman and Paleologus dynasties. The greater part of these were in such a *délabrement* that it was impossible for those in the interior of the Saray to use them, so badly ordered were they and so *confondus pêlemêle*. . . . Therefore the sultan [Ahmed III] built the Library and put there the manuscripts which were in the Imperial Treasury.[47]

During the years when the Grand Seraglio was forbidden territory — an inaccessibility which continued
for more than a half century after the palace ceased to
be the residence of the sultans — many attempts were
made by scholars to obtain knowledge of the contents
of this library, in the hope that survivals from the imperial library of Byzantinium, from that of Matthew
Corvinus and others, might be found, but always without success. When access became possible, it was only
to find that a large part of the once vast collection had
been dissipated, and that the remainder, in so far as the
items have been identified, comprised none of the great
lost treasures of the past.

In the pursuit of the present study a list of books has
been found which is believed to be an accurate copy of
the catalogue of the Seraglio library.[48] This list is included in the *Sulla litteratura turchesca* of the Abbate
Toderini, published in Venice in 1787. The Abbate,
erudite Jesuit and orientalist, was in Constantinople
from October 1781 until May 1786, in the capacity of
tutor to the son of Constantino Garzoni, Venetian *bailo*
to the Sublime Porte. Originally interested in collecting
coins and manuscripts, he conceived the idea of writing
a history of printing in Constantinople with a catalogue
appended of those books which had been translated into
European languages, and vice versa. From that developed the further idea of including also accounts of
the studies of the Turks, their academies and their
libraries, and lists of the books in these libraries. To
this end he was especially desirous of obtaining a copy
of the catalogue which he was told existed of the Arab,
Persian, and Turkish books in the library of the Grand

Seraglio. Failing after many attempts to enter the palace in disguise, he finally attained his end,[49] as he relates it, in the following manner:

A seigneur among my friends who is now in Madrid and who is sufficiently connected with Turks of high rank, at the end of forty days procured the catalogue of the Library for me, which was copied by one of the pages in the greatest secrecy, writing a few lines day by day. The undertaking seemed not only difficult, but impossible to persons who know the Serai.

That it is genuine, he continues,

is shown by the fact that it has no connection with the lists of other libraries in Constantinople, but is of a totally different type, and almost unique, for it does not deal with grammars and dictionaries, etc., which are useless books for the library of a sovereign. Instead there are books on Religion, the Sciences (Knowledge), many Histories, books on Moral Philosophy, Politics, Urbanity, many of which are not found in public libraries, but are well suited for the *purpose of education*, of the Emperor, and for the culture of the Serai. In final proof some of these are so rare and so little known even by scholars that the page, if he were not transcribing them, could certainly not devise them.[50]

Toderini adds that he has preserved among his oriental manuscripts the copy of the catalogue made from the original of the *Saray*, which is in Turkish and in Turkish characters. The translation of the titles, which is also included along with the Turkish text of the catalogue in the *Sulla litteratura turchesca*, he says, "was made at my request by the learned Signor Cavaliere Cosmo Comidas, Dragoman of the Kingdom of Spain." The catalogue is divided into the following categories: commentaries on the Koran and traditions; books on jurisprudence, philosophy, logic, astronomy, geometry,

arithmetic, medicine, and moral philosophy; and books
ascetic or contemplative.

It is thought by some musicologists that the Turks
are indebted to the Arabs for their keen appreciation of
vocal music, for many of their musical instruments, for
the extensive use of wind instruments in the open, and
for the theory and the technical nomenclature of their
music.[51] Following the conquest of Constantinople,
Turkish music is said to have received a second foreign
impulse from the Greek composer Caharias,[52] and a
third when Murad IV in 1638 took Baghdad and conveyed to his capital Shah Culi (?), "the Orpheus of
Persia," and four other musicians.[53] Chiefly under the
patronage of the sultans it continued to develop until
it reached its culminating point under Selim III and
Mahmud II, who were themselves performers and composers of some note. Although the first musician of
the palace (*Sazendeh Bashi*) during the reign of Murad
IV had been a celebrated musician, in the third quarter
of the seventeenth century the Turks still had no knowledge of the system of notation then in vogue in Europe.[54]
In 1691 Prince Demetriu Cantemir studied Turkish
music and wrote a learned treatise on the subject, making use of notes, it is said, for the first time, but about
a century later Toderini says that "the theory of Turkish music, being different beyond expression, the Turks
have abandoned notes and again compose and perform,
according to their ancient custom." [55]

The account of the music of the Grand Seraglio given
by Albert Bobovi is historically valuable not only as a
detailed description of the palace music of the seventeenth century but also as a reflection of Turkish music

in general of the same period. The majority of Turks, it is said, were devoted to music, which, as among the Greeks, was considered a part of a liberal education.[56] The art of Turkish music, according to Bobovi, was a combination of the melody, the touch of the performer, and especially his ability to extemporize. Both chamber music [57] and military music were taught in the Palace School. Chamber music consisted largely of vocal music. The length or brevity of the line of a song invariably determined the meter, of which there were twenty-four types in Turkish music. One verse, the measure and cadence of which strongly resemble the Alexandrine, but for which a masculine form of rhyme was invariably employed, was used especially for improvisation, a form of music always especially popular with Turks.[58] There were three types of Turkish songs: lyrical, philosophical, and folk songs. The *chansons délicieux*, or lyric songs, of which there were four subdivisions, the *Murebba*, *Kiar*, *Nat*, and *Semay*, were written for the most part in Persian and were the songs of the "erudite and civilized." The poet Vasuf (?) Osman Bey (ob. 1240 A.H. or 1824/5 A.D.), who was educated as a page in the Palace School, was one of the most famous composers of songs of this type. The second class were the *chansons spirituels* (*sic*), or philosophical songs, of which there were three subdivisions, the *Tesbih*, *Ilahi*, and *Tevhid*. The third class consisted of the folk songs, or songs of the common people, called Türkü,[59] which were composed in accented syllabic strophes, the strophe numbering two, three, four, lines (usually three) and the line from seven to fifteen syllables, and which treated of war, victory, love (often in the form of dialogue), suffering in the absence of a loved one and other familiar emotions, and humorous themes of Ramazan.

The principal instruments used to accompany the lyrical and philosophical songs, according to Bobovi, were the *kemenche*, a type of little viol; the *santur*, or psaltery; the *miskal*, or bagpipe; the *nefir*, or Persian bagpipe; the *nay*, or flute; the *ud*, or lute; and the *tanbur*, or *sheshtar*, or *qitara*, a lute type with three strings and a very long neck having a large number of frets for marking the tones and semitones,[60] which was played not with the fingers but with a plastrum of tortoise shell, or with a quill. Instruments used to accompany folk songs were for the most part three-stringed, such as the *chaghaneh*, the *thschegour (chugur?)*, the *tanbur*, and other simple instruments of the people. The usual instruments used for military music are said to have been suited for the pomp of ceremony rather than for military exercises. These instruments were the *buru* or trumpet; the *davul*, or ordinary drum, and a special variety of large bronze drum which, mounted upon a horse, was used to announce the approach of the sultan; the *naqareh*, consisting of several copper plates which were beaten one against the other; and the *kumdum (qudum?) betcke (sic), dunbalek*, and *lil (zil?)*, all of which were varieties of cymbals.[61]

The Conservatory of Music (*Meshq Khaneh*), which is said to have been especially well furnished and well adapted in every way to teaching purposes,[62] was not a separate unit like the other vocational schools of the Grand Seraglio but a school for all members of the student body. With the exception of a certain number of the masters of military music who were required by the nature of their duties to be constantly present in the palace, and who were lodged in the Hall of the Expeditionary Force, the music masters were nonresident. During the forenoon the building was given over to chamber music, and in the afternoon to military music. Pages who specialized in chamber music were trained in both solo and chorus parts. As palace musicians their duties do not appear to have been onerous; each Tuesday they gave a concert while the sultan's hair was being cut or other rites of his toilet performed. On rare occasions, blindfolded and closely guarded by black eunuchs, they gave concerts for the harem, the harem music as a rule being supplied by the young girl slaves and the black eunuchs.

The guild of military musicians, which numbered three hundred, had their quarters at the Iron Gate, one of the sea gates in the outer wall of the Grand Seraglio. From an early period the military band is reported to have played at the royal palace at the time of the *Ikindi*, that is, the third prayer of the day, which is said in the middle of the afternoon.[63] Its other functions were to salute the sultan a half hour before dawn and one and a half hours after sunset, and to accompany him whenever he appeared in public; to sound the *reveillon* two hours before sunrise, and the curfew two hours after sunset, upon certain towers of the city; to announce the two *Bayrams*; to serenade the embassies on their principal fete days; and to honor those pages who had completed the course of the Palace School with the title of pasha or *beylerbey*. In 1612 there are said to have been one hundred and fifty members of the military

band.[64] It was the candid opinion of Bobovi that Turkish military music was no more than "a fracas, a great
and disagreeable noise." On the other hand the Jewish
page Habesci, while conceding that it was without
doubt barbarous from the point of view of noise, was of
the opinion that "it had enough of sweetness and harmony to make one like it." [65]

As soon as the pages were of an age to endure strenu-
ous physical exercise, no effort was spared to render
them strong, agile, and courageous.[66] Initial physical
exercises were the lifting and carrying of heavy weights.
The apparatus of the first exercise consisted of a pulley
and cord fastened against a wall, with a bag attached
to the end of the cord, which at first weighed from six
to ten *oqas* * and was later increased to thirty-five and
even forty *oqas*. A page drew the cord with his right
hand while bracing his left against the wall. The second exercise was the lifting and carrying of various kinds
of weights in the arms and upon the shoulders. The
first weights were the heavy timbers used for firing the
furnace of the Bath of the Inner Palace, which the pages
carried upon their shoulders. From time to time the
size of these timbers and other weights was increased
until, it is said, pages in the upper halls were frequently
able to carry as much as three hundred and seventy or
even three hundred and eighty *oqas* for a distance of one
hundred and fifty, or one hundred and sixty paces.
Later iron weights of various kinds were substituted.
It is said that the pages were able with one arm to lift
weights which ranged from forty to one hundred pounds,

* An *oqa* is the equivalent of about two and three-quarters pounds
avoirdupois.

and that those which they were able to raise above their heads were "almost unbelievably heavy." For the fifteen pages who stoked the bath furnace (who were almost certainly from the Great Hall) there was a special apparatus consisting of three iron bars

fasten'd upon great Cramp-Irons over the door that goes into the Baths, and the middlemost of the three, as it is commonly reported, weighs a hundred *Okkas*, which amount to Three hundred and fifty pounds, *Paris* weight, an *Okka* weighing three pounds and a half, or thereabouts. There was heretofore one of these *Ichoglans*, of so prodigious strength, that the Grand Seignor himself would have the satisfaction of seeing a tryal, whether he could with one hand lift up and turn about that Iron-bar; which he did to the great astonishment of the Prince, and presently after he entertain'd him with another demonstration of the strength of his Arm. Over those three Iron-bars, there hung two Head-pieces of Iron, whereof one was an inch in thickness, and the other about the eighth part of an inch. The same *Ichoglan* did, in the Grand Seignor's presence, at one blow of a Battle-Axe, cut through the head-piece of an inch thick, and at one blow with a Sabre cleft the other to the middle of it.[67]

Each year, during the festivities which accompanied the celebration of the first *Bayram*, competitive tests in the lifting and carrying of weights were attended by the sultan and the entire personnel of the Palace School. In the course of the tests the military band played and the onlookers acclaimed their favorites with the cry of "Allah, Allah, give him strength." The winner received a purse of five hundred *écus* * from the sultan and, in certain instances, was promoted to the Hall of the Treasury.

* An ancient issue of currency which varied in value at different times from three to six *livres*.

More advanced physical exercises were archery, wrestling, sword practice, and *chomaq* (*chelik chomaq*, a game played with a wooden ball attached to a cord)[68] and *jerid* (dart throwing, the players being on horseback). The magnificent quivers of the sultans, richly overlaid with diamonds, emeralds, and other precious stones, which now form part of the permanent exhibition of the Imperial Treasury, offer convincing testimony of the high esteem in which archery was held by the Turks as a sport, even after it had ceased to be important as a means of warfare. Murad IV, who performed prodigious feats with the bow and arrow, especially encouraged this sport. Pages of the Palace School received their first instruction with a bow strung with a chain. From practice bows of this type they were promoted to bows strung with sinew, the most advanced of which required very great strength and skill to draw. Yet even with the largest and heaviest of these bows the record of two hundred draws without stopping is said to have been not infrequent at the school matches and tournaments. Several sultans, especially Sultan Ibrahim, greatly enjoyed wrestling as a spectacle and encouraged it among the school sports. The pages anointed their bodies with oil in the customary manner and wrestled nude, except for their shorts (*calecons*). Before entering the arena, they invariably offered up a special prayer for wrestlers which ran as follows: "Allah! Allah! For the sake of the Lord of all created beings — for the sake of Muhammad Mustafa, for the sake of Muhammad Bokhari of Sari Saltiq,[69] for the sake of our sheykh Muhammad who laid hold of the garments and the limbs, let there be a setting-to of hand upon hand, back upon back, and breast upon breast! And for the love of Ali, the Lion of Allah, grant assistance, O Allah!" Another popular exercise was a kind of sword and buckler practice originally introduced from Poland. A page held in his left hand a pad shaped in the form of a shield, and in his right hand a scimitar with which he practised a driving blow calculated to sever the head of a sheep or the foot of a dead camel. Of the energy with which the pages entered into these games it is said by the author of the *Serai Enderum* that "they made more noise than all the laqueys of Paris, of which I am able to speak with authority, as I live in Pera close by Galata Saray and I vow to you that I sometimes think that all the devils are shut up in this seminary and that they hold their general chapter there." [70]

Since the majority of the students of the palace schools were destined for the cavalry service, one of the main lines of physical training was fine horsemanship, which was especially encouraged by Suleiman I. Not only did the pages become skilled cavalrymen, but they also excelled in feats of horsemanship. While running their horses at full speed, they would unsaddle and re-saddle them without slackening their pace; they would ride standing on the seat of the saddle; they would ride two horses at the same time with one foot on each saddle; two pages while riding at top speed would exchange horses with one another; and they would slide under the bellies of their horses and remount from the other side.

The game of *jerid*, which was played in the *jerid* field, a large "piazza" situated on the Marmora side of the palace, near the place where once had stood the *Nea*,

or New Church of Basil the Macedonian,[71] was a mock
battle in which mounted horsemen threw wooden darts
at each other. Although it attained its greatest popularity in the period between Muhammad IV and Mustafa II (1695–1703), it was a prominent feature of royal
entertainment in the Hippodrome at least as early as
the second half of the sixteenth century. In his state
papers, William Harborne, ambassador from Queen
Elizabeth to Murad III and first to hold that post, has
left an interesting description of a game which he witnessed in the month of July, 1582:

On Monday 9 [July, 1582], after dinner there appeared in
the Piazza, the King's falconer, the son of the said Achmet
Bassa and many important gentlemen [pages], who skirmished together throwing darts against one another using one,
two, three, and four at a time, they were mounted on most
beautiful horses splendidly caparaisoned and changed them
after every two or three courses, shewing themselves as
dexterous and quick at throwing the dart and evading those
of the enemy, that they were reputed to be brave knights
which was done thus because of the presence of the King and
the Sultans. The Son of the Governes [aïa] of the Sultana
Mother, much loved and favored by her also taking part. . . .
Tuesday the 10th, there were no more than 80 horses, beauti-
fully caparaisoned who began skirmishing at midday, and
continued till the evening throwing darts in the Romish fashion as was done yesterday but with greater show of wounding
one another, those of yesterday being persons of quality having restrained themselves. When night came the usual fireworks were displayed in the presence of the Signore, the
Mother, the son, the wife, and the Sultanas. Wednesday
close on a thousand persons paraded round and round the
hippodrome with the braying of drums, lutes, flutes, and other
instruments in use among them, making a great noise, and
one may say singing with great discordance, and after going

round the Hippodrome two by two, they left. Then came the Signores wrestlers who naked gave very fine trials of strength and dexterity, each endeavouring to overcome the other, to obtain the victory, there was a prize bestowed by B . . . of thousand aspres. Then having left there appeared certain spahi on horse-back, who skirmished with darts, which took up the rest of the time. . . . Wednesday the twelfth the morning passed quickly but after dinner a hundred horse appeared and performed in divers ways, besides tilting with darts. . . . On the following days till the 18th nothing further happened, but at the twenty-fourth hour, the same horse appeared to skirmish and wound each other with darts till evening, when the usual fireworks were displayed for five or six hours continuously.[72]

It is said that Muhammad IV delighted so much in the game that

every one in hopes of preferment, and in emulation one of the other, endeavoured to be a Master in it, and most are become so dexterous, that they will dart a stick of above three quarters of a yard long with that force, that where it hits, it will endanger breaking a bone. The Grand Signore every day passes his time with seeing his Pages exercised in this sport, in which ordinarily one knocks another from his Horse, and seldom a day passed in which some receive not bruises or desperate wounds. This Sultan doth many times appoint days of combat between the Black Eunuchs and some of his White Pages on Horseback, in this manner with the Gerit; and then happens such a skirmish with such emulation, each side contending for the honour of his colour, race and dignity, with that heat and courage, as if they contended for the Empire; this pastime seldom concluding without some blood.[73]

During the first years of the reign of Mahmud II the game was still played by the pages "during *Bayram* and at every other possible opportunity, although everyone,

old and young, knew that it no longer served the purpose
of training for war, and that it was a dangerous game.
But because it once had been considered so fine a game,
no one dared to say a word against it." Mahmud II
abolished it at the same time that he abolished the
Janizary corps, "an action which sorely discontented
the black eunuchs, who were great advocates of it because it was so good a show." [74]

Of the introduction of vocational training into the
curriculum of the Palace School at the end of the preparatory period, Rycaut says: "To the former Lessons
of School learning and exercise abroad, are added some
other accomplishments of a Trade, handy-craft, or
Mystery." [75] The pages of each of the four schools of
vocational training specialized in the particular "Mystery" of that school. The pages of the Hall of the Expeditionary Force, who constituted the military band of
the Inner Palace and accompanied the sultan when he
was on campaign or traveling, received special training
in music, in the arts of laundering, and in the care of
the royal accouterments; those of the Hall of the Commissariat were taught to prepare the royal beverages
and specifics which were dispensed from the Privy
Commissariat, and were the actual cupbearers to the
sultan; those of the Hall of the Treasury were charged
with set duties in connection with the Imperial Treasury
and its contents; while those of the Hall of the Royal
Bedchamber performed the offices of the royal bedchamber and were also entrusted with the care of the
holy relics. Additional vocations in which large numbers
of pages were instructed were falconry and attendance
upon the bath. Pages to the number of seventy or

eighty, of whom the twelve senior ones were drawn from the Hall of the Treasury and the remainder from the Hall of the Commissariat, were trained to accompany the sultan upon his hunting expeditions. Forty pages, taken from different halls at different periods, were attached to the bath of the Palace School, twenty-five as attendants within the bath (*dellaklar*), and fifteen as stokers of the bath furnace (*kulkhanjiler*), four of the stokers remaining always on duty in a chamber adjoining the furnace (Plan I, 19). Besides this common bath, each of the halls had a separate bath, with shifts of pages from the hall in attendance upon it. Twice each day the first officer of the bath (*hamamji bashi*), who was nominally attached to the Hall of the Expeditionary Force but who was actually inspector-general of the palace baths, made the rounds of the entire school and instructed the attendants in giving baths and in keeping the baths in order. It was also the duty of this officer to inspect the clothing of the bathers in order to see that it was neat, clean, and free from insects of every kind. Shaving, manicuring, and the arrangement of the turban, which were formerly a part of the ceremony of a Turkish bath, were performed not by the pages in attendance upon the bath but by mutes and dwarfs stationed in a chamber between the bath and the small mosque belonging to the Great Hall. At the feast of the first *Bayram* the bath attendants received for their services each the sum of one thousand *aqchas*, in addition to their regular allowances as pages.[76]

At the height of the Palace School, the instruction is said to have been excellent. The Italian *bailo* Ottaviano Bon writes in 1608: "I was told that it was amazing with what diligence and solicitude the students of the Palace School were taught." As the empire declined, and with it learning in general, the quality of the instruction also suffered, but so effective was the practical organization of the school that the palace system of education continued, without apparent diminution of its power, for a much longer time than the slave system of government of which it was the main support.

CHAPTER V

THE SEPARATE SCHOOLS OF THE GRAND SERAGLIO

THE nine palace schools — five preparatory schools and four vocational schools — formed a closely correlated system of education. At the same time each of the schools was a separate and self-subsisting unit. As has already been stated, the three outside, or auxiliary, schools of Adrianople, Galata *Saray*, and Ibrahim Pasha, were preparatory schools for the Great and Small halls, while these two halls were in turn preparatory to the three vocational schools, the halls of the Expeditionary Force, of the Commissariat, and of the Treasury.[1] From any one of these three, students were promoted to the Hall of the Royal Bedchamber. After the abolishment of the auxiliary *sarays*, novices were put directly into the Great and Small halls, and there were even instances, like that of Evliya Efendi, of students being admitted directly into one of the professional schools. Like Evliya, the distinguished Grand Vizir Soqullu Muhammad Pasha is said to have entered directly into the Hall of the Commissariat, and to have held two court offices, those of steward of the Privy Commissariat and of first gatekeeper, before being transferred to the government service. Kiuprulu Muhammad Pasha, Albanian by origin, and the first of the line of grand vizirs of the Kiuprulu dynasty, through the kindly offices of a compatriot employed as a confectionery cook in the kitchens of the

Grand Seraglio, also gained admission to the same hall. Later transferred to the Hall of the Royal Bedchamber, he was promoted to the position of master of the royal horse, and from that to the governship of Damascus. Qibrisli (Cyprian) Mehmed Pasha was taken directly into the Hall of the Treasury through the influence of his uncle, Mehemet Efendi of Cyprus, who was steward of the Imperial Treasury.

During the period when the Palace School was at its height, the full course of training extended over an average period of fourteen years. After serving a novitiate of seven or eight years in any one of the auxiliary schools, the pages were promoted to either the Great Hall or the Small Hall, or else were permitted to leave the auxiliary schools with the rank of *Sipahis* of the reserve corps. As the number of students in each of the four vocational schools was small and rigidly limited, only a relatively small proportion of those who entered the preparatory schools were promoted to any one of the schools of vocational training, and a still smaller proportion completed the entire course, the majority being sent out to inferior posts in the army and government upon the completion of the preparatory school course. The curriculum of each school was therefore carefully planned, not only with a view to promotion from one school to another in hierarchical order but equally with a view to appointment to military and civilian posts of corresponding grade.

Under Muhammad II promotions from one school to another are said to have taken place "when the pages had been in the School a certain time, or when in the opinion of the sultan he felt that he could trust them."

At a later period the chief white eunuch, as director-in-chief of the palace system of education, made the circuit of the palace schools every two or three years [2] for the purpose of promoting students and, at the same time, of dismissing "all those whom he thinks incapable of doing their Prince good service, or betray their disgust of so austere a life." The promotion of a student having been decided upon, one of his officers conducted him to the threshold of the new hall, where he gave him a blow upon the neck with his thumb, and introduced him to his new officers. The student was then assigned a place known as the "Place of the Lastcomer" (Plan II, 2) and given the most menial tasks of the hall to perform.

Between the students of the preparatory schools and those of the vocational schools there were marked distinctions. The preparatory students, who were called novices or apprentices (choqalular),[3] performed no personal services for the sultan and were clothed in simple wool and linen [4] — hence their additional designation as chuqalular, or those clothed in wool. After the establishment of the English Levant Company, their garments are said to have been of "good English Cloth and Linen, neither fine nor coarse." The pages of the four upper halls enjoyed the enviable distinction of being the personal servitors of the sultan and were therefore bedecked in "Satten Vests and Cloth of Gold," and as an additional mark of distinction were permitted to wear the long coat known as the qaftan — hence their designation as the qaftanlilar.

The main difference between the Great Hall and the Small Hall, as the names indicate, was one of size. In the sixteenth century the Great Hall had a capacity of from one hundred to two hundred students.[5] In the middle of the following century six hundred or more students were housed in the two halls, four hundred in the Great Hall and two hundred or two hundred and fifty in the Small Hall.[6] In the second half of the same century, after the general reduction in the size of the court which took place under Muhammad IV, the total number in the two halls as given by Hezarfen Husein Efendi was four hundred and sixty-eight, of which two hundred and eighty-five were in the Great Hall and one hundred and eighty-three in the Small Hall.[7]

There appears to have been also a slight variation in rank from time to time between the two schools. In the sixteenth century the more immature students were grouped in the Small Hall.[8] In the seventeenth century the situation appears to have been reversed, the students of the Great Hall suffering certain disqualifications which indicate almost surely that it was they who were the more immature of the two; as their allowance they received only seven or eight *aqchas* per day, whereas the pages of the Small Hall received from ten to twelve;[9] they were not served from the kitchen of the chief white eunuch, as were the pages of the Small Hall and the noncommissioned officers of their own hall; they, alone of all the pages, were not served the regulation dish of *pilav* on Thursdays;[10] and — very probably in order to relieve the congestion in the mosque of the Inner Palace where the other students of the Palace School, including those of the Small Hall, went for the *namaz*, or five daily prayers — the students of the Great Hall had a small mosque of their own to which they went for the first four prayers of the day (Plan I, C), remaining in their own hall for the fifth.

The course of study in all five preparatory schools

extended over an average period of from six to eight years.[11] As the average age of admission was from twelve to fourteen years, the preparatory period corresponded almost exactly with the years of adolescence. Given this formative period with which to work, the main problem was to transform youths of alien race and religion into loyal Turks and Moslems, a transformation rendered imperative by reason of the fact that a large proportion of the students were sent out from the schools at the end of the preparatory course. The curriculum of the preparatory schools was carefully planned to this end. It was thoroughly characteristic of the emphasis which the Turks — "the gentlemen of Europe" — put upon etiquette that from the first day of their matriculation the pages were taught "silence, reverence, humble and modest behaviour, holding their heads downwards, and their hands across before them." [12] Their registration having been completed, they were introduced to the officers of their hall, the position of each official at the same time being carefully explained to them. They were next introduced to the older pages, whose hands they were directed to kiss,[13] a sign of inferiority in the Orient. Whenever high officials entered the third court, they were preceded by a court functionary making a loud noise, in order to give the novices time to run and hide, since they were not permitted to remain and salaam as the older students were.[14] From the beginning the novices were also drilled in the elaborate ritual of the five daily prayers, and in the tenets of the Moslem faith.[15] Within the first five or six days they began to speak, read, and write Turkish, an intensive study of which was continued for about four years.[16] During the course of the first year they also began the study of Arabic. Physical training, which played so large a role in the curricula of the professional schools, was begun in the preparatory schools, with archery, wrestling, running, jumping, and the lifting and carrying of graduated weights.[17]

The Hall of the Expeditionary Force (*Seferli Oda*), the lowest in rank of the vocational schools, at the time of its establishment by Ahmed I was composed of pages drawn from the Great and Small halls. Thereafter such average graduates of these two halls as continued the work of the Palace School seem, for a time at least, to have been promoted regularly to this hall, while those who gave signs of more than usual promise were promoted to the halls of the Commissariat and Treasury. At a later period there does not appear to have been any such differentiation. The number of pages of the Expeditionary Force ranged at various times from seventy or eighty to one hundred and fifty.[18] As the name of the hall indicates, they accompanied the sultan whenever he quitted the Grand Seraglio, whether in residence in some other of the royal palaces, traveling, or upon campaign. At such times they were charged, as has already been said, with the cleaning and repair of the royal accouterments and with the washing of the royal linen — hence the occasional appellation of the Hall of the Launderers.[19] When the sultan was in residence at the Grand Seraglio, the pages of the Expeditionary Force were held responsible only for the ceremonial laundering of the royal turban, the remainder of the royal linen being regularly laundered by palace domestics. Each Tuesday a chorus from the Expeditionary Force stood, heads lowered and hands crossed, and discoursed music, while the first officer washed the muslin of the imperial turban in a silver basin, hung it in front of the Hall of the Expeditionary Force to dry, and later folded and scented it. The five senior pages of this hall were invariably attached to the suite of the chief white eunuch, and four to the suite of the sword-bearer.[20]

The term of study of the Hall of the Expeditionary Force was five or six years. At the time of their admission the pages were taught to dress and to arrange their turbans in the manner of young Turkish gentlemen. They were also instructed how to shave, how to manicure, and how to perform other rites of the toilet properly. As befitted their higher rank, their allowance was increased from eight *aqchas* per day to ten or twelve,[21] and the manner in which they were housed was more spacious and imposing. The following inscription, which was evidently removed from the Hall of the Expeditionary Force at the time that it was reduced in size by Sultan Abd ul-Mejid and which was in 1928 one of a heap of detached and broken inscriptions piled in a corner of the second court near the Divan, records the enlargement of the hall by Ahmed III:

His Majesty Sultan Ahmed III
Within his Kingdom the Light of the Sun,
He, the Ghazi, Shah of the Throne of Happiness, is the
    Worker of Wonders,
He, the Guardian of Goodwill, is famous for his learning,
    kindness and favors,
He who in all things is worthy to be preferred above his royal
    ancestors,
He who has exerted his power beneficently,
He who, surpassing all else, built the Library of the Palace —

Such that he only who has gazed into the Crystal has beheld
    its equal —
To him the *Seferli Oda* [Hall of the Expeditionary Force] in
    its need appeared as a vision,
Like old age, contracted, narrow,
Its inhabitants suffering, the strong as well as the weak.

II

He hastened to give his *Firman* [royal edict] for its rebuilding.
Let His Name be praised so long as the world endures;
Let us pray for the Ruler whose abundant favor gave the
    Seferli Oda.

III

When the Moon of the East appears, morning and night,
Let a *Halim* (?) be his reward.

IV

Let the Servants of the *Seferli Oda* attend hourly,
For it is they who are appointed to pray.

V

Let God permit Him to remain the Same during his reign
And make His Heart happy in both worlds.

VI

Fa'iz was witness of its rebuilding and recorded the date
That Sultan Ahmed renewed the *Seferli Oda.*

While it has been difficult to ascertain the exact stages
at which new subjects were added to the curricula of the
four upper schools, it seems likely that it was in the Hall
of the Expeditionary Force that the study of Persian
was begun, together with the reading of "divers au-
thors" in this tongue and in Turkish and Arabic. It was
in this hall also that physical training first became definitely military in character and acquired the importance

which it continued to have in the other three professional schools. The chief exercises introduced at this
period were cavalry practice, the game of *jerid*, the use
of the dart and saber, and the throwing of stones. Following the suppression of the Great and Small halls by
Muhammad IV, physical training was begun in the Hall
of the Expeditionary Force, and became necessarily
somewhat more elementary in character.

It was also in the Hall of the Expeditionary Force
that a page began to learn the craft in which it was
"held an honor rather than an ignominy" to be skilled.
The pages of the Expeditionary Force usually learned
sewing, embroidery, leather work, the making of bows,
arrows, and quivers, and the repairing of guns.[22] But a
more important subject of study, characteristic of the
hall, second only to the arts of war and of government,
was music. Although no information has been found
as to the amount of musical instruction received by the
pages of the Expeditionary Force, there is considerable
evidence that the Hall of the Expeditionary Force was
more closely linked than any other hall with the Conservatory of Music. The Conservatory was situated
next to this hall (Plan III, 22), and a number of singers
and dancers were lodged there, as well as some music
masters, including the head music master. After the
first officer of the Expeditionary Force, the head of the
baths and the head music master ranked respectively
as the second and third officers of the hall. That the
pages of the Hall of the Expeditionary Force had the
reputation of being especially devoted to music is shown
by an incident that occurred during the reign of Mahmud II, which is related by Hafiz Elias Bey. Orders

had been given by the sultan that none of the palace
pages should be allowed to play or sing without his express permission. Yet it was known that, in spite of
this rule, the discipline was now so relaxed that every
three or five days certain of the pages were accustomed
to gather and to play and sing in the Hall of the Expeditionary Force:

Now it happened one evening after the last prayer of the
day, when these light-hearted men were gathered to hear
Sonjolju [Plumber] Zadeh Salih Efendi sing, sacrificing their
very souls to listen to his melodious voice, that the soot in
the chimney, under the influence of the passionate sighs of
these lovers of music and beauty, caught fire, at first slowly,
and then rapidly, until the roof also caught. The alarm being given, all the pages came and worked, each as if he were
trying verily to save his own hall. When the Sword-bearer
arrived, he restrained himself and did not enter the burning
hall, as it was the custom that outsiders should not enter.
Fortunately the fire was extinguished before great harm had
been wrought, before even the beds had taken fire. Having
been informed of this good news and having rewarded those
who had extinguished the flames, the Sword-bearer rebuked
the First Officer of the Expeditionary Force in the presence
of his pages, a proceeding which was unheard of and which
was regarded as a great insult to the First Officer. He like-
wise criticised the Custodian of the Keys to such a degree that
the Custodian grew as red as a beet. Having ordered everyone present to be henceforth more careful and having for a
second time thanked those who had assisted, the Sword-
bearer withdrew to the Royal Bedchamber.[23]

Students who left the Palace School upon completion
of their course in the Hall of the Expeditionary Force
were given commissions in the halberdiers (*baltajilar*),
in the Imperial Guard (*Muteferriqahs*, literally "quarter-

masters"), a picked corps of from one to two hundred officers who were mostly Ottomans in the second generation, or in the cavalry corps of the Sublime Porte (*Sipahis*).[24] In the early period those who continued their course seem to have been promoted, according as aptitudes developed and vacancies occurred, either to the Hall of the Commissariat or to the Hall of the Treasury. When the Palace School was at its prime, the average age of admission to these two halls was twenty-two years, and the average length of the course of study in each four years.[25]

The amount of time given to vocational training in both the Hall of the Commissariat and the Hall of the Treasury was greater than that in the Hall of the Expeditionary Force, while the emphasis upon academic work and physical training does not appear to gave been greatly diminished. As a case in point may be cited the programme of Evliya Efendi during the time that he was a page in the Hall of the Commissariat. Besides the large amount of time which he gave to the study of music, and that which must always have been required for physical training, he had lessons in Persian and Arabic grammar and calligraphy, and three lessons a week in the Koran. In common with the remainder of the student body, he attended the nine public lectures which were given weekly by the most distinguished professors of the Palace School.

The Privy Commissariat [26] was the storehouse, the "secret dispensary," for drugs and articles de luxe for the royal harem and *selamlik*. Here were stored a full assortment of drugs, above all of potent antidotes for poisons; the rare and costly spices, perfumes, and aromatics brought from Egypt, Arabia, and the Indies; the huge candles brought from Wallachia for lighting the selamlik, harem, and palace mosques; vast quantities of jams, marmalades, and other sweetmeats; a supply of drinking water from the two Chamlijas and from the spring of St. Simon in the Old Palace; the delectable syrups, manufactured to order in "Grand Cairo," which were the foundation of many of the royal drinks; and the great pieces of ambergris, sent by the pasha of the Yemen, which was one of the ingredients of a favorite variety of sherbet.[27]

The number of pages in the Hall of the Commissariat (*Kiler Odasi*) was one hundred at the time of its establishment by Muhammad the Conqueror,[28] forty in the sixteenth century,[29] and variously seventy, eighty, and from one hundred to one hundred and ten in the seventeenth.[30] The pages' duties in connection with the Privy Commissariat were varied and manifold. They kept it in order; prepared the favorite sweets and sauces of the sultan; molded and distributed the ordinary candles in use in all apartments of the palace, exclusive of the royal apartments; and, finally, manufactured and dispensed to the public on behalf of the sultan, in order that he might win the recipients' prayers, the pastilles and amulets of amber and musk in great demand as aphrodisiac talismans, and the one-half ell lengths of *taffeta ciré* employed for the dressing of wounds.[31] From ten to thirty pages, who as a rule were drawn from the Hall of the Commissariat, and the Chief Commissary, who was charged with this duty in the Code of Laws of Muhammad II, attended the sultan during the serving of his meals.[32] As cupbearers of the sultan, they mixed and served the "exquisite drinks," the sherbets, juleps, and manifold others which under the restrictions of Islam were the substitutes for stronger potions. Every day six messengers, three pages from the Hall of the Commissariat and three water-carriers of the Grand Seraglio, were dispatched to the "Fountain of Saint Simon" to obtain drinking water for the use of the sultan. Six flagons, each of which contained twenty ounces, were filled with this water, sealed with red wax, returned to the Grand Seraglio, and stored in the Privy Commissariat for the sultan's individual use.[33]

When the Grand Seignor is thirsty, and calls for water, the Page of the *Haz-Oda* [Royal Bedchamber] immediately makes a sign to the two pages of the *Kilar* [Commissariat], of whom one advances up to the *Kilar-bachi*, or Cup-Bearer himself, crying out *Sou*, which signifies Water, to advertise him, that the Prince would drink; and the other runs to the door of the *Haz-Oda*, where the most ancient of the Forty Pages gives him Ten *Sequins*. That Page is the Treasurer of the said Chamber, and he pays the small Sums which the Grand Seignor gives order for, an Officer which might be call'd in *English*, the *Treasurer of the petty Enjoyments*. The Water is sometimes brought in a Cup of Gold, sometimes in a Vessel of Pourcelain, placed upon a large Server of Gold, about two foot diameter, and enrich'd with Precious Stones within and without. That is look'd on as one of the richest pieces of Plate belonging to the Seraglio. The principal Cup-Bearer, who is a white Eunuch, carries it with great Ceremony, attended by a hundred pages of the *Kilar*, whom he ordinarily has under his Charge, and upheld under the Arms by two of them, who walk on both sides of him. For it is requir'd, That he should carry it lifted above his head, and so he cannot see his way but by looking under it. When he is come to the Door of the *Haz-Oda*, the Pages of the *Kilar*, who have accompany'd him so far, pass no further,

save only the two who uphold his Arms, and the Pages of the
Chamber go along with him quite into the Grand Seignor's
Presence. But when they come to the door of the Chamber,
two of the more ancient among them, take the places of the
two Pages of the *Kilar*, and compleat the conducting of the
Kilargi-Bachi [Head of the Hall of the Commissariat], under
the Arms, to offer the Cup to the Prince. When he has not
anything to say to him, he carries it back again into the *Kilar*;
but if he will take his opportunity to entertain him with some
Affair, he delivers the Cup and the Server into the hands of
one of the Pages, who led him under the Arms, and he delivers it to those, who, belonging to the Cup-Bearer's Office,
waited there in expectation of his return.[34]

The Imperial Treasury was not, as has often been
erroneously asserted, the actual state treasury; the
only revenue directly received there was that from
Egypt and the adjacent provinces,[35] and no periodic
disbursements were made from it. It was the great
repository of the booty of war, surplus wealth, and rich
gifts accumulated by the sultans from the foundation
of the monarchy. At the height of the Ottoman power,
this treasury was popularly supposed to be one of the
seven wonders of the world, its riches incalculable and
its treasures without price.[36]

With the exception of the reigns of Muhammad II and
Muhammad IV, when it was about one hundred,[37] the
number of pages of the Hall of the Imperial Treasury
was maintained steadily at sixty,[38] the highest average
of any one of the four vocational schools. The pages
of the Treasury were distinguished from the other pages
by a rich bonnet which is estimated to have been worth
from one thousand to twelve hundred ducats.[39]

With the exception of the quarterly cleaning of the

Winter Chamber, with which they were charged,[40] the duties of the pages of the Treasury were limited strictly to the care of the Imperial Treasury and of its contents. They assisted in the elaborate ceremonies which always attended its opening. Upon the receipt of an order for its opening, the pages assembled in the Hall of the Treasury, formed in procession, and marched behind the head treasurer to the central door:

the first thing that is done is the untwisting of a Chain, which they had put there, for the better securing of the Seal, which the Chief Officer of the Treasury had set over the hole, and having found it entire, he orders it to be broken by the keeper of the Keyes, and commands him to open. As soon as they are got into the Chamber into which the *Chaznadar-bachi* knowes they are to go, he sets himself down upon a low Bench, and declares what Piece it is that the Grand Seignor requires. They [the pages] thereupon open the Coffer, wherein it ought to be, then they present it to the *Chaznadar-bachi* [Head-treasurer] . . . whatever is receiv'd into the Treasury, and whatever goes out of it, is exactly set down and en-roll'd by the *Haznaquatib*, or Clerk, who keeps the Registers. . . . As to the little Chest or Coffer, wherein the most pre-cious Jewels are kept, it is impossible to get anything out thence; for when the Grand Seignor would have any Piece taken out of it, he orders the Coffer itself to be brought into his Presence, by the principal Officer of the Treasury, accom-pany'd by the Keeper of the Keyes, and all the Pages; and before he opens it, he takes notice whether the Seal be entire. After he has taken what he desir'd, the Coffer is lock'd up in his Presence, the Seal is set upon it, and is carry'd back into the Treasury with the same Ceremony. Then do the Sixty Pages receive, ordinarily, some demonstrations of the Grand Seignor's Liberality, which may amount to ten or twelve *Purses*, to be divided amongst them.[41]

An inventory of the contents of the Treasury, even of the smallest *objets d'art*, was kept with minutest care in the registers of the Treasury.[42] Whenever articles were given out for use in the palace, the sword-bearer, into whose custody articles from the Treasury were always delivered, was required to give the head treasurer receipts for them. At the death of a sultan the head treasurer made an inventory of the contents of the Treasury in order to ascertain if everything which had been given out during the reign had been returned. It was the custom to make an inventory also in the event of the appointment of a new head treasurer, and at the same time to sell any useless and broken articles. These articles were sold at auction outside the palace by those halberdiers-with-tresses who were attached to the Treasury, and inside the Gate of Felicity by the pages of the Treasury. Once a year also, during the months of June, July, and August, six of the pages of the Treasury known as "old-clothes men" (*dellatlar*) auctioneered at the doors of the different halls [43] the discarded garments of his Imperial Majesty and those confiscated from pashas condemned to death. Whenever in the discretion of the head treasurer it was deemed necessary, the pages dusted the coffers of the Treasury, and inspected and cleaned the textiles, furs, clothing, and other articles stored in them.[44] Among these precious articles were the ancient garments of the first Ottoman sultans, made, like those of the Angora shepherds of today, of sheepskin *à petit poil frisés* and of white felt painted with colors. Here also were kept the state garments of the sultans. Twice a year these robes were thoroughly cleansed and sunned by the pages of the Treasury.

Whenever gold to the amount of two hundred purses (*keyseh*) had accumulated in the outer chambers of the

Imperial Treasury, the grand vizir notified the sultan, who thereupon appointed a day for transferring it to the secret vaults underneath the Treasury. Tavernier has left us a picture of this ceremony:

The day being come, the Grand Seignor, led under the arm by the *Chaznadar-bachi* [head treasurer], who is on the left-hand, which is accounted the more honourable amongst the Turks, and by the *Seligdar-Aga* [sword-bearer], who is on the right, comes into the Chamber of the Treasury, where the Sixty Pages expect him, ranked in order on both sides, with their hands cross their Breasts. The Grand Seignor, having pass'd through the Chamber, and order'd the first Door of the Secret Treasury to be open'd, enters into it, by the light of several Torches of white Wax, and is follow'd by the Pages, two by two, till they are within the Vault, into which the Bags are brought, ty'd with a Silk-string. Upon the string they put a piece of red soft Wax, whereto the Grand Seignor sets his Seal himself, which is upon a Gold-Ring . . . after which they put the Bags into the Coffers, which are all double chain'd.[45]

In the early period of the monarchy it was the custom to seal the Imperial Treasury with the seal of the reigning sultan, but from the reign of Selim I until the deposition of Muhammad VI in 1922 it was sealed with the seal of Selim, which bore his seal (*tughra*) and the inscription, "Trust to a high destiny." This sultan, who filled the coffers of the Treasury to overflowing with gold coin, was reported to have said, "Whoever fills with copper the Treasury which I have filled with gold, may seal it with his own seal," in consequence of which no one of his successors was ever so bold as to make use of his own seal.[46] Since the establishment of the Turkish Republic the Treasury has been sealed with the new seal

of the republic, bearing the familiar crescent and star
of the Turkish flag.

At the time of the establishment of the Hall of the
Royal Bedchamber by Muhammad II, it numbered
twenty, and later in the same reign thirty-five, pages.[47]
During the first half of the following century the number
at times soared as high as fifty and fell as low as eight
or ten.[48] It was finally fixed at forty in the second half
of the sixteenth century,[49] and remained at that figure
during the rest of its history. (It is an interesting fact
that in 1928 the Angora government still retained forty
curators in the Pavilion of the Holy Mantle.) The number being thus strictly limited, the principle of survival
of the fittest, which prevailed at every stage of promotion in the Palace School, was most rigidly applied at
the time of admission to the Hall of the Royal Bedchamber. When vacancies occurred promotions were
made from the Hall of the Treasury and, to a less degree, from the halls of the Commissariat and Expeditionary Force, pages who were not promoted usually
receiving appointments to the *Muteferriqahs*, or to the
Boluks, a squadron of the cavalry,[50] both of which corps
made part of the bodyguard of the sultan. That the
system of merit continued in force, at least nominally,
until the abolition of the Palace School as a school of
state, may be inferred from an instance cited by Hafiz
Elias Bey. Upon one of the occasions of the return
of the court from the summer palace in Beshiktash,
Mahmud II,

after having gone to the Pavilion of the Holy Mantle and
thanked the Almighty for a safe return, inquired of the First
Officer of the Royal Bedchamber if any vacancies existed

in his hall. Upon the reply that one vacancy did exist, the
sultan demanded a list of the eligible pages. Those whose
names were presented to the sultan as holding the required
ranks and as having attained the necessary grades, were the
Master of the Wardrobe in the Hall of the Treasury, the
Master of the Towels in the Hall of the Commissariat, and
the Head Launderer in the Hall of the Expeditionary Force.
From such a list, it is the custom of the sultans to choose
those pages who have the finest physique and most pleasing
manner.[51]

It is said that the final test for admission to this hall
was one of loyalty to Islam.[52]

As the attendants closest to the person of the sultan
and as the custodians of the holy relics, the pages of the
royal bedchamber enjoyed certain privileges and bene-
fits denied to other pages of the Palace School. At the
time of their admission to the Hall of the Royal Bedchamber they were presented with a purse of two or
three thousand *aqchas*, several costumes of cloth of
gold and silver,[53] and an increased allowance, which was
eighteen or twenty *aqchas* in the sixteenth century, and
forty in the seventeenth, as compared with the eight or
ten and ten or twelve *aqchas* respectively of the pages
in the other vocational halls.[54] Upon the rare occasions
when they were sent upon confidential missions, student
officers also received gratuities from the pashas of Wallachia, Moldavia, Transylvania, and the Khan of the
Crimea.[55] They were permitted to converse freely with
the palace people and to walk in the palace gardens
during recess.[56] Punishments could be administered
only with the knowledge of the sultan and in the presence of the sword-bearer, and were limited to scolding
or to light blows on the back of the neck. In the late

period of the Palace School, while the pages of the royal bedchamber were, without exception, required to be present at the principal meal of the day and nominally resided in the Hall of the Royal Bedchamber, they were permitted to maintain homes and families in the city and upon stipulated occasions to go to them.[57] One of the sword-bearers of Mahmud II owned a farm near Belgrade Forest and entertained lavishly there, entertaining the sultan several times and also the British ambassador.

Besides the first officer of the royal bedchamber (*hass oda bashi*), who was sometimes a white eunuch but more frequently a page,[58] there were five titular officers in the sixteenth century: the sword-bearer of the sultan; the master of the wardrobe, who ranked second after the sword-bearer, and as the insignia of his office always carried the royal raincoat in a wrapping of flaming red; the cup-bearer; the bearer of the royal shoes; and the bearer of the royal seat, a large low portable stool, usually covered with cloth of gold and embroidered with pearls and other stones.[59] The sword-bearer, who was usually selected for his good looks and who took his title from the fact that he carried the sword of the sultan sheathed in a red scabbard, although only a page was also first chamberlain of the court and one of its most important officers. He was always in attendance upon the sultan when he held audience in the Rooms of His Presence. In individual instances where a sword-bearer had particularly distinguished himself, he was granted the right to be present at the ceremonies which attended the celebration of the birthday of the Prophet. Under the Code of Laws of Muhammad II he was entrusted

with the discipline of the novices, an office that carried
with it the right to inflict corporal punishment (*silleh
chalmaq*). He was also one of the masters of petitions,
in which capacity he presented the petitions of the pages
to the sultan. In 1648, the sultan appointed the sword-
bearer, Suleiman Agha, directly to the office of grand
vizir. The office of sword-bearer was abrogated upon the
death of Silahdar Ali of Crete in 1247 A.H. (1831/2 A.D.).

In the course of the seventeenth century the offices of
bearer of the royal shoes and bearer of the royal seat
were done away with, and thirteen others were added,
which were as follows: the first squire, who, when the
office was first created, was the superior of the master of
the wardrobe, but later became his inferior; the bearer
of the turban of state; the custodian of the keys of the
royal bedchamber; the first barber; the ewer-bearer;
the first and second custodian of the napery; the master
and the assistant master of the kennels; the keeper of
the parrots; the first manicurist; and two others, the
kahuchji (*qaushji*? bearer of the shawl or waistband)
and the *hilatdgy* (*halatji*? maker, or tender, of the cord
or rope), titles which, because of the peculiar transliteration, it has been impossible to identify with any degree
of certainty.[60] The first squire, the sword-bearer, and
the master of the wardrobe alone had the right to wear
a turban, all the other pages of the royal bedchamber
having gold embroidered bonnets. Together with the
sword-bearer and the master of the wardrobe, the first
four of the above officers always appeared in public
with the sultan; they also received larger allowances
than the officers who were their inferiors in rank, and
they had the additional title of master of petitions (*arz*

aghalari), which carried with it the right to present petitions to the sultan and to accept rewards for so doing,
and the privilege of using the common room, or smoking
room, of the white eunuchs who held the same title
(Plan I, 18), and of sharing their hospital ward [61]
(Plan I, 53). The remaining ten officers, who were without individual insignia of rank, wore, as a common
badge of distinction, a kind of dagger or knife in a gold
sheath, by reason of which they were known as *bichaqli
eskiler*, or elders with knives. Of these the seven lowest
in rank, in addition to the sword-bearer, attended the
sultan in the Rooms of His Presence.[62] The remaining
pages, who were without titles of any sort, performed
the more menial services of the royal bedchamber.

So great was the mystery and ceremony with which
oriental monarchs of the past were accustomed to hedge
themselves about that little knowledge of their intimate
daily life, even of the most famous of them, has come
down to posterity. A single picture appears to survive
of a Turkish sultan in the Hall of the Royal Bedchamber.
Evliya Efendi relates that shortly after his assignment
as a page to the Hall of the Commissariat he was summoned in audience by Murad IV. He continues:

One day they invested me with an embroidered dress, put
an amber-scented tuft of artificial hair upon my head, and
wishing me a thousand blessings, told me I had the crown of
happiness on my head. . . . On the day I was dressed as
above related, with the splendid turban, two mutes came,
and with many curious motions led me into the *Khas oda*
[Inner Chamber] to Melek Ahmed Agha and his predecessor
Mustafa. These greatly encouraged me, and taught me
several new expressions and ceremonies, which I was to observe in the presence of the emperor. I now found myself in

the Khas oda, and had an opportunity of examining it. It is a large room with a cupola; in each corner there are raised seats or thrones; numerous windows and balconies, fountains and water-basins, and the floor is paved with stone of various colours, like a Chinese gallery of pictures. The emperor [Murad IV] now made his appearance, like the rising sun, by the door leading to the inner harem. He saluted the forty pages of the inner chamber and all the Musahib [associates] who returned the salutation with prayers for his prosperity. The emperor with great dignity having seated himself on one of the thrones, I kissed the ground before it, and trembled all over. The next moment, however, I complimented him with some verses that most fortunately came into my mind. He then desired me to read something. I said, "I am versed in seventy-two sciences, does your majesty wish to hear something of Persian, Arabic, Romaic, Hebrew, Syriac, Greek, or Turkish? Something of the different tunes of music, or poetry in various measures?" The emperor said, "What a boasting fellow this is! Is he a Revani [a prattling fellow], and is all this mere nonsense, or is he capable to perform all that he says?" I replied, "If your majesty will please to grant me permission freely as a Nadim [familiar companion], I think I shall be able to amuse you." The emperor asked what the office of a Nadim was: "A Nadim," said I, "is a gentleman who converses in a pleasing manner: but if he is permitted to drink with the emperor, he is called Nadim nab [Nadim-i nab], or companion of the glass. Nadim is derived from Monadamat, and by a transposition of letters, we have Mudam, which in Arabic signifies pure wine. If such a Nadim is permitted to enjoy the company of the emperor, he is called Musahib [intimate companion]." "Bravo," said the sultan, "he understands his business, and is no Revani." "Revani indeed," replied I, looking at the same time towards Yusuf Pasha, the late Khan of Revan (Erivan). The emperor struck his knees with his hand, and burst into such a fit of laughter that his face became quite red; then addressing Emirguneh, his favorite musician, he said: "What do you think of this devil of a boy?" Yusuf Pasha said: "Mark this youth, he will very soon astonish all Iran and Turan, for his eyes are constantly dancing." "Yes," said I, "the eyes of Turkish boys dance in order to excite mirth in strangers." I alluded to Emirguneh, who, when he was in a good humour, frequently danced and played. The emperor laughed and said, "The boy has ready answers," and being full of good humour, he ordered some chakir to be brought. Chakir in his metaphorical language signified wine. He drank a glass, and said, "Evliya, thou art now initiated into my secrets; take care not to divulge them." I replied by the following verses:

> "Deep in thy breast be love's secret hid —
> Forbid thy soul to feel its presence there, —
> And when death hovers o'er thy darkening lid,
> Still in that knowledge let no other share!"

. . . "Evliya," said the Sultan, "having spoken so much of science, let us now hear some of your performances in music." I enumerated all the different tunes . . . and he then ordered me to be dressed in a fur robe. Seeing that it was too long for me he said, "Send it to thy father that he may remember me in his prayers"; and he directed that another should be given me. He next with his own hands put on my head a sable fur-kalpak. Before this I had had only a plain Tatar kalpak. He then desired me to sing a warsiki [mystic song]. . . . In obedience to the sultan's orders, I took up a *dayara* [tambourine], and kissed the ground before the sultan. On looking at the dayara, he observed that it was set with jewels, and said, "I make thee a present of this dayara, but take care thou dost not go beyond this circle." I leaped in a sprightly manner, kissed the foot of the throne . . . I then seated myself on my heels as usual, offered up a short prayer for assistance from God, and after several symphonies, I exclaimed, "O thou Sheik Gulshani, tutor of my tutor Dervish Omar Raushani, hail!" I now began to sing and dance, turning round in the manner of the Dervishes, and accompanying with the dayara, the following warsiki [mystic song] composed by Dervish Omar for the late Musa,[63] whose situa-

tion I had just entered; with a low and plaintive voice I
sang:

"I went out to meet my beloved Musa; he tarried and
    came not,
  Perhaps I have missed him in the way; he tarried and
    came not."

On hearing this plaintive song, the Sultan took up his pocket
handerkerchief, and when I approached him, he turned round
and said: "The boy has brought to life the spirit of Musa
Chelebi! Now tell me the truth instantly, who told thee to
sing this song, which I have forbidden to be sung in my
presence, and who taught thee it?" I replied, "My emperor,
may your life be prolonged. My father had two slaves who
learnt the song from the writings of Irmaghan Mohammed
Effendi, who died during the late plague, and from them I
learnt it. I have heard it from no one else, nor did any one
tell me to sing it in the presence of my emperor." The Sultan said, "The boy is very ingenious; he quotes the authority
of dead men, that he may not compromise the living." He
then said, "Mayest thou live long," and desired me to proceed with my performance. . . . I then stood silent, and
having kissed the ground before the emperor, he praised me
highly, and gave me several pieces of gold. . . . In the evening
he ordered me to read a tenth of the Koran; I commenced
where I had left off the holy night of Kadr [Night of Power]
at Aya Sofia, that is, at the Sura Aa'raf (al-Araf?), and read
two hundred and four verses, divided into two makam,
twenty-four sha'ba, and forty-eight tarkib. I then repeated
the names of the Sultans Ahmed, Othman, and all their illustrious ancestors, to whom I transferred any merit I might
have had from this reading of the Koran, and concluded
with the Fatihah [first chapter of the Koran]. The Sultan
then presented me with a fish-bone belt set with jewels,
which he had in his hand. . . . At this moment the Mu'azzins
began to call prayers at the head of the staircase, which looks
toward the courtyard of the palace. The emperor ordered
me to assist them. I flew like a peacock to the top of the

staircase, and began to exclaim, "Hai a'la-as-salah! i.e. Ho! to good works."

After this first exhibition of his talents, Evliya says that, because of intense preoccupation with his studies, "it was but seldom I could attend in the service of the emperor, but whenever I came into his presence he was always delighted, and treated me so graciously, that I never failed to show my wit and pleasantry. I should never have been tempted to repeat any of my witty sayings, but for the express command of the Sultan." [64]

CHAPTER VI

DAILY LIFE; CEREMONY OF DEPARTURE; APPOINTMENTS

IN ITS requirements of seclusion and celibacy, the palace system of education in its strictest days closely resembled the monastic system of the West. Upon admission, the pages were severed from all connection with their past, not only being cut off from all communication with their families, but in general losing all track of them and even of their own identity; in a few instances only, notably those of the Grand Vizir Ibrahim Pasha and the Grand Vizir Soqullu Muhammad Pasha, is it recorded that a page continued to maintain relations with his family after entering the Grand Seraglio, or renewed relations with them upon leaving it. Once within the walls of the palace, the pages were isolated, even from one another. Conversation, except the necessary intercourse with the officers of the hall, was permitted only at stated intervals. Communication of every kind between the different halls was strictly forbidden.[1] Every possible precaution was taken to prevent intercourse between the pages and the outside world. Necessary errands in the city were executed by official messengers, who were required to obey a page's slightest wish or command so long as it did not infringe upon the school regulations.[2] At the time that Angiolello and Menavino were in the palace, this corps was composed of twenty gatekeepers, and at the time of

Bobovi of one hundred and twenty "apprentices of the
Outer Service." Only under very special circumstances
could a visitor obtain permission to see a page, and then
always in the presence of two or more white eunuchs.[3]
With the exception of the first four officers of the royal
bedchamber, who invariably attended the sultan when
he appeared in public, and of the pages of the Expeditionary Force, who accompanied him whenever he
quitted the Grand Seraglio, the pages of the superior
schools were permitted to go out of the Grand Seraglio
only when they went to practise at the field for archery
(*oq meydani*) on the upper stretches of the Golden
Horn, when they appeared in public games in the
Hippodrome, when they attended the sultan on occasions
of unusual state, and, in instances rarer still, when they
were dispatched on highly confidential missions to
provincial officials.[4] Pages of the two preparatory
schools never passed beyond the Gate of Felicity except
to attend the school sports in the field of archery and
dart practice in the Outer Palace or, in the event of ill-
ness, to go to the infirmary in the first court, to which
they were conveyed in a closed litter. It was popularly
believed that the majority of the student body never
saw a woman from the time they entered the Grand
Seraglio as young boys until they left it as mature men,
and that some of them did not even remember what a
woman looked like.[5]

The pages of the Palace School, like all the other corps
of palace attendants, wore a distinctive costume. It
was marked by a similarity in cut rather than by the
use of any one color or combination of colors, and with
the exception of the *qaftan* worn by the students of the

four upper classes and of a difference in the headdress
worn by the pages of the two superior vocational schools
— the embroidered hood attached to the *qaftan* of the
pages of the royal bedchamber and the rich bonnet of
the pages of the Treasury — it was the same for all the
halls. It consisted of the wide baggy trousers known as
shalvars, a gilded girdle, boots of soft red or yellow
leather attached to the trousers, and a high headdress
which was exchanged during study hours for a skullcap
(*taqyeh*).[6] Thomas Dallam, an Englishman and master
organist who was engaged in setting up in the palace an
organ presented by Queen Elizabeth to Murad III, on
one occasion while he was at work saw a troop of pages
pass by, and describes their appearance thus:

200 were his principall padgis apparaled in ritche clothe
of gould in gowns to the midlegg, upon their heads little caps;
great saches of silk about their wasites; on their legges red
cordovan buskins. Their heads all shaven saving behind
their eares a locke of hare like a squirrels taile. Very proper
men & Christian borne.[7]

Although in the early period the pages of the Great
Hall wore a scarlet uniform,[8] in general the choice of
color seems to have been left to the individual taste, except that black was avoided [9] and that the pages of the
royal bedchamber usually wore cloth of gold or cloth
of gold and silver. The pages were not permitted to
crop their hair or to grow beards, which were signs of
free birth among the Turks; and it is said that after the
fashion of Joseph, slave of Pharaoh, who was their
patron saint, they were required to wear tresses at each
side of their turbans in order that they might be perpetually reminded that they were slaves. The tresses of

novices were worn in a line with the tips of their noses, while those of the older pages came to their chins.[10] In line with his military reforms, and his general tendency towards modernization, Mahmud II abolished the ancient style of the pages' dress. It is recorded by Hafiz Bey that upon the ninth day of Ramazan, 1244 A.H. (1829), the sword-bearer, having completed the registration of the pages, delivered to them the imperial order that thereafter, instead of the *qaftan* and skullcap, they must wear the zouave, *shalvars*, shirt, and fez with tassel, in conformity with the Egyptian fashion.

The daily schedule of the student body was organized with the same elaborate care as was the central administration of the Palace School. Each hour had its appointed task. Two hours before the first prayer, which took place about dawn, the officers of the day summoned, with three strikes of a hammer upon a plaque of iron suspended from a column in each hall, the pages whose turn it was to perform certain duties connected with the halls or the bath. The remainder of the pages were called in the same manner an hour before dawn in winter, and a half hour before dawn in summer. A half hour after each call the same officers made the rounds of the halls; if upon the third round a page was not yet out of bed, his bed was drawn out from under him; if he were late for the prayer he was scolded; and, in the case of a repetition of the offense, he sometimes received corporal punishment. When the toilet of everyone had been completed, the night officer of each hall, flanked at either side by an assistant, recited a prayer for the safety of the reigning sultan and the repose of the souls of the dead sultans, and for the guidance of the Ulema, those in authority in the palace, and in the empire. The prayer finished, a gong was sounded three times as the signal for the pages to take their positions, each beside his bed, for the calling of the roll. Then, remaining "marvellously silent," each page rolled, tied, and suspended from a hook on the wall the large heavy coverlet which did double duty as mattress and covering; he then placed his pillow underneath, and put in position the small chest (*cassette*) which was the substitute for a desk, upon which two lighted candles were placed by the pages on duty for the day. While awaiting the muezzin's call — the column of porphyry about six feet high which may still be seen in the third court served on this occasion as a minaret — a page carefully selected for his beautiful voice read aloud from the Koran. As soon as the call sounded, the pages formed in double line and marched, with heads lowered and hands crossed upon their breasts, to the mosque of the Palace School. The deportment of the pages at this time is said to have been "an admirable sight to see." At four o'clock Turkish, which was four hours after sunrise, the first meal was served. This finished, classes and other school work began and continued until the serving of the second repast. Then followed a quiet hour, during which the outer doors of all the halls remained closed. From the close of the quiet hour until the third prayer there was a short afternoon session. During the hour which preceded the sunset prayer, and again before the fifth and last prayer of the day, the pages, having performed their ablutions, seated themselves and read the Koran. The time for retiring, which the officer in charge of a hall announced by striking a cane upon the floor, immediately followed the return from the mosque after the fifth prayer. The roll was again called, the marks of the day were entered, and the punishments, which appear to have been cumulative until this hour, were administered.

During the festivities which attended the two *Bayrams*, this routine and rules in general were almost entirely relaxed. Dressed in their finest raiment, the pages attended the *baise-main* held by the sultan upon these occasions and kissed the hem of his garment. Having received his gracious permission, they were free to entertain themselves day and night for four days.[11] At one other time only were the ordinary routine and discipline of the Palace School in abeyance — when a page was confined in the school infirmary. Except in the matter of diet, which is said to have consisted entirely of bouillon and tiny morsels of fowl,[12] and which, the page Bobovi complains, was of a nature to make ill the most vigorous, there was great freedom and indulgence in the infirmary. Song and instrumental music were supplied all day long. The law of prohibition enjoined by the Moslem religion and strictly enforced in other parts of the palace was also greatly relaxed. While prospective patients were forbidden to carry alcohol in any form into the infirmary — an offense for which, if caught, they received three hundred strokes or paid a fine of three hundred *aqchas* — so long as they remained within the infirmary precincts, by a curious circumlocution of law and logic, they were permitted to imbibe freely. This ruling led to the rise of a class of smugglers — in this case the palace gardeners — who by means of ropes hoisted rubber canteens filled with wine and other strong drink over the wall between the outer garden and the infirmary.[13]

Under these conditions, it is not strange that a page immured for a decade or more within the palace walls looked upon a period of residence in the infirmary not as a penance or hardship but rather as a diversion and holiday. To prevent too-frequent visits to the infirmary, the rules regarding admission, as given by the page Menavino, were very strict. Before a page could be moved from his hall, it was necessary for his physician to apply to the sultan for permission to make the transfer, and, in event of its being granted, the physician was required to visit his patient four times a day. In the seventeenth century, when the general discipline of the palace was considerably relaxed, no such restrictions were placed upon the admission of patients. But woe betide the unhappy physician who should make a mistake in diagnosis! The penalty was, literally, an eye for an eye, and a tooth for a tooth. For example, the tooth of a page could not be pulled without the express permission of the sultan; should the extraction prove to have been unnecessary, the physician then and there suffered the loss of one of his own teeth.[14]

Judged by the standards of the time, the fare provided for the pages was sufficient in quantity and wholesome, even if monotonous in the extreme. There seem to have been two principal meals in the day, each of the six schools being served in its own hall, with the exceptions only of the superior officers, who were served in their own apartments. The menus of these two meals were identical and appear to have been always the same, a boiled mutton without sauce of any kind (*suyush*), a daily dole to each page of two thin loaves of bread, and several varieties of soup served in rotation. These were cheese soup, lentil soup, and cream soups thickened with rice, honey, and saffron, or with rice, honey, and currants, or with flour and currants. At the second meal on Thursdays *pilav* was served to all the pages, with the exception of the novices in the Great Hall.[15] Commenting upon this fare, Sir Paul Rycaut, who had an extensive knowledge of Turkish conditions based upon seventeen years' tenure of official positions in different parts of the empire — but, let it be remarked, no first-hand acquaintance with the fare in question — reflects philosophically that it "becomes the Table of Scholars, where there is nothing of superfluity, as there is nothing of want." On the other hand, it is in keeping with the universal student character that Albert Bobovi, who as a page had firsthand acquaintance with this diet, should have complained of it with great bitterness.

The ideals, requirements, and proscriptions of the Palace School in matters of etiquette, deportment, and dress explain in large measure why the Turks have always enjoyed so high a reputation for courtesy and good manners. The essential aim of the training was to inculcate in the pages a deep loyalty and reverence for the sultan. They were taught to refer to him always with the greatest reverence, and when in his presence never to look in his direction, but to bow the head and to cover the eyes, to keep the arms folded or the hands crossed, and to preserve perfect silence. In general they were enjoined to comport themselves with dignity, to walk sedately — fancy steps in marching especially being forbidden. They were instructed to dress in a manly fashion, especially not to wear effeminate colors; to have their clothes always well pressed, the *qaftan* buttoned, the underwear clean, and a fresh pocket handkerchief every day. It was required that a page should take a bath and have a manicure and pedicure once a week, should shave at least twice a week, and have the hair cut once a month. He must supply himself with fresh towels, both hand towels and foot towels, and a piece of soft cloth for the ears, every two days. It was anathema to manicure in public or to splash water upon others in the bath. A page was forbidden to begin eating until after his superiors had been served, to look hungrily at the food, to eat in haste or with the mouth full, or to partake of onions or garlic. Above everything else, Allah forbid that he should belch or hiccough during a meal! His mouth and hands must always be washed immediately after each meal. He must show consideration for his neighbor in smoking. It was forbidden him to yawn, to stretch his limbs, to scratch himself, or to hunt for fleas or other insects in public. The proper manner of blowing the nose, expectorating, and sneezing was prescribed in detail. Among the pages themselves it was a rule of courtesy that a seat in which a handkerchief or rosary had been placed was *balta* (probably *balta ahmak*, meaning "reserved"), and it was esteemed discourteous to take it.[16]

Only a small proportion of the pages, probably from one-eighth to one-fourth, as has already been said, completed the full course of study of the Palace School, the majority either being sent out from the school at the end of the preparatory period, or, for personal reasons,

petitioning the sultan for appointments before completing the course.[17] The average age of graduates in the
sixteenth century was from twenty to twenty-five
years,[18] and in the seventeenth and first half of the
eighteenth, from thirty to forty.[19] In the last century
of the school's existence the length of the course became
indefinite, pages in the lower schools rarely soliciting
appointments, or even *congé*, except for the purpose of
retirement.[20]

The departure of the pages from the palace is said by
Rycaut to have been accomplished

with as much ceremony and complement [*sic*] as is exercised
in the most civil parts of Christendome. For though the
Turks out of pride and scorn, comport themselves to Christians with a strange kind of barbarous haughtiness and
neglect, they are yet among themselves as precise in their
own rules of complement and civility, as they are at *Rome*,
or any other parts of the civilized world.[21]

Those who were about to take their leave first repaired
to the throne room, where the sultan awaited them
upon the threshold, the pages kissing his hand and he
in turn bowing to them. Following this exchange of
salutations the sultan made an address in which he
urged them to discharge zealously the duties of the
offices to which they were about to be sent; to be loyal
to their sovereign; to hold inviolate everything that
they had seen and known during the time that they had
been in the palace, especially "those things which had
offended their sense of right and justice," and, above all
else, to remain faithful and devout Moslems. In concluding he presented each page with a robe of honor, a
golden headband containing three or four hundred gold

ducats, the sum of about one thousand silver *aqchas* tied in a handkerchief, and as many pages and horses as befitted the post to which he had been appointed.[22] The grand vizir, other high officials, and wealthy eunuchs also presented money and slaves.[23] The queen-mother, whose retinue on the occasions of her public appearance included eight pages from the Palace School, and other women members of the royal family gave gifts of vests, linen breeches, and handkerchiefs richly wrought and of great worth, and often of their own handiwork.[24]

Upon quitting the presence of the sultan the pages proceeded to take farewell of their fellow students. In the event of an appointment to the high post of *beyler-bey*, a quantity of silver *aqchas* placed in two huge silver cups or vessels was conveyed by two eunuchs to either side of the Petition Kiushk. To fanfares and blasts of music from the palace band, the eunuchs threw the coins, and immediately thereafter the cups, among the pages of the Great Hall and Small Hall. The pages scrambled for them, passing the cups from hand to hand like a football until they were finally thrown over the goal, which in this case was the group of students of the upper classes (*qaftanlilar*), the cups becoming the property of those pages who had thrown them over the goal. It is said to have been "a marvellous pleasure" to see the dexterity with which the cups were handled. If the appointment were to a post lower than that of *beylerbey*, the page himself scattered coins among his fellow pages on his way out of the palace.[25]

From the Gate of Felicity the chief white eunuch and the palace intendant conducted the pages to the Imperial Gate (*Bab-i Humayun*), on the threshold of which

the chief white eunuch proceeded to deliver some last
words of counsel and good will. This over with, the
pages kissed the hands of these officers, and of those
other high officials of the palace who were present and
of the *Agha* of the Janizaries, mounted their horses, and
rode off to the palace of the grand vizir, scattering
aqchas as they went. Having paid homage to the grand
vizir, they were then free to go into retirement for a
period of from three to five days, or to dispose otherwise of the time as they saw fit, while their beards were
allowed to grow.[26]

A page who thus rode forth into the outside world had
been ennobled for life by the service which he had performed for the sultan and by the training which he had
received. He was certain of high pay and steady employment; he was exempt from taxes and imposts of
every kind; [27] and he had open to him opportunities for
advancement to which there were no limits save his
own merit and the sultanate itself. Although the *cursus
honorum* in the Ottoman system was not absolutely
fixed — as is shown in the case of Ali Pasha who, from
the position of gatekeeper in the Outer Service of the
Grand Seraglio, was promoted to that of head-taster
and later to the regular cavalry, ultimately becoming
grand vizir — in general it followed a fairly regular
pattern.[28] A chosen few of the pages were retained in
the Grand Seraglio and promoted to the higher branches
of the court service. The most promising of the pages
from the halls of the Treasury, Commissariat, and Expeditionary Force received appointments in the Imperial Guard (*Muteferriqas*), or by the sultan's favor

one might be made head gatekeeper of the palace, or royal taster (*chashnigir*).[29] Others received appointments in the feudal cavalry,[30] or were transferred to the Outer Service as messengers of state (*chavushes*). The majority from these three schools, however, including those sent out in the retinues of newly appointed officials, received appointments in the regular cavalry, or cavalry of the Sublime Porte (so called in contradistinction to the feudal cavalry), which, together with the Janizaries, constituted the two crack divisions of the Turkish army. A typical example is Evliya Efendi, who, after two years as page in the Hall of the Commissariat, served as a *Sipahi* in the expedition against Erivan in 1636, with an allowance of forty aspres per day. The regular cavalry, which were all included under the general name of *Sipahis*, or horsemen, were, according to Professor Lybyer, subdivided into four corps as follows:

the *Spahis* in the narrower sense, often called *Spahi-Oghlans*; the *Silihdars*, or weapon-bearers; the *Ulufagis*, or paid troops, in two divisions, the left and the right; and the *Ghurebas*, or Foreign Legion, also in two divisions, the left and the right. ... In Suleiman's time the actual number of the four corps counted from ten to twelve thousand men, or a little less than the number of the Janissaries; but since most of them had each to bring from two to six additional horsemen, the total force which they assembled was from forty to fifty thousand.[31]

Sir Paul Rycaut picturesquely describes the arms, particular function, and pay of the *Sipahis*:

These light Horse-men are armed with their Scimitar and Lance, called by them *Mizrak*, and some carry in their hands a *Gerit*, which is a weapon about two feet long, headed with Iron, which I consider to be the same with the *Pila* amongst

the Romans, which by long exercise and custom they throw
with a strange dexterity and violence, and sometimes darting
it before them in the full career of their Horse, without any
stop recover it again from the ground: they also wear a
straight Sword named *Caddare*, with a broad blade fixed to
the side of their Saddle, which, or the Scimitar, they make
use of when they arrive to handy-blows with the Enemy;
many of them are armed with Bows and Arrows, and with
Pistols, and Carbines; but they esteem not much of fire-
Arms, having an opinion, that in the field they make more
noise than execution: some of them wear jacks of Mail and
Head-pieces painted with the colour of their Squadron; in
fight they begin their onset with *Allah, Allah*, and make three
attempts to break within the Ranks of the Enemy, in which
if they fail, they then make their retreat. . . . Their duty
in the War is to stand Centinel with a *Janizary* at the end of
every cord at the Grand Signiors Pavilion, as also at the
Vizirs, armed with his Cemitar, Bows, Arrows, and Lance,
mounted on Horse-back; as the *Janizary* on foot with his
Sword and Musket and also the charge of the Treasure for
payment of the Militia, is committed in the field to their
custody. . . . Their pay is diverse, but in general it is from
twelve to a hundred Aspres a day: those who proceed from
the *Seraglioes* of *Pera, Ibrahim Pashaw*, and *Adrianople*, which
are so many Nurseries and Schools as well of the principles
of War, as literature . . . have the lowest pay of twelve
Aspres a day; but those who are extracted from the less, or
greater Chamber of the Grand Signiors own *Seraglio*, called
Seni [Yeni] serai, have 19 Aspres pay, and if they are fa-
voured with the title of an Office, they receive two or three
Aspres augmentation. . . . But such as are elected to the
War out of the more eminent Chambers, as the Landery, the
Turbant Office, the Dispensatory, the Treasury, the Falconers Lodge and others (which we have mentioned in the Description of the *Seraglio*) have, at first, thirty Aspres daily
pay: an encrease of which is obtained sometimes by the
Viziers, or Registers favour unto two Aspres more; sometimes
by services in the War, by receiving two Aspres augmenta-

tion for the head of every Enemy he brings in; two Aspres more for intelligence of the death of any *Spahee*, out of the pay of the deceased; as also at the Incoronation, or Instalement of every Grand Signior, five Aspres increase is given as a donative general to the whole Army of *Spahees*: and thus many of them by art, industry, and good success go augmenting until they arrive to a hundred Aspres, and here is their *non plus ultra*, they can rise no higher.[32]

The *Sipahis* occupied a very high position. Writing of them in 1534, Benedetto Ramberti said: "They always journey, and also encamp, at the right hand of the Signor. They are a great people. From them the Signor is wont to choose his chief men. They are first put as boys into the palace, and when they grow up they succeed well if they attain this grade; it is like a ladder to mount to higher positions." Bishop Paolo Giovio writes four years later:

As to the cavalry, those called *Spahi-oghlani* or *Spahiglani* [Cavalry-pages], these are the flower and élite of all, because they have been reared within the place called "The Enclosure" [*Enderun*] and instructed in letters and in arms in the same manner as the children of the Prince Sultan. They are put some in the cavalry ranks and some with the infantry, and in these consist all the strength of the Turks. Also they serve the lieutenants and governors of the provinces in honorable and profitable matters, and from these are appointed the sanjak beys, who are held in such high esteem that they are married to women of the royal blood. These are the noblest and best loved by the prince, being the best mounted and the best accoutred in rich furs and skins, and the first in order of all those who are with the Turk. . . . They are one thousand in number, each of which has servants from the number of three or four to ten, and the said *spahis* wear hats on their heads as do the others and cloth of gold brocade or velvet of purple or other color. Their office is to accompany the Grand

Signor at his right side and at all times when he goes out of the city.[33]

Busbecq has left a vivid description of the appearance presented by the *Sipahis* upon the occasion of Suleiman I's departure for Anatolia to punish his rebellious son Bayazid:

I was accommodated with a window at the back of the house, commanding a view of the street by which the Sultan was to pass. From this I had the pleasure of seeing the magnificent column which was marching out. The Ghourebas and Ouloufedgis rode in double, and the Silidars and Spahis in single file. The cavalry of the Imperial guard consists of these four regiments, each of which forms a distinct body, and has separate quarters. They are believed to amount to about 6000 men, more or less. Besides these, I saw a large force, consisting of the household slaves belonging to the Sultan himself, the Pashas, and other court dignitaries. The spectacle presented by a Turkish horseman is indeed magnificent. His high-bred steed generally comes from Cappadocia or Syria, and its trappings and saddle sparkle with gold and jewels in silver settings. The rider himself is resplendent in a dress of cloth of gold or silver, or else of silk or velvet. The very lowest of them is clothed in scarlet, violet, or blue robes of the finest cloth. Right and left hang two handsome cases, one of which holds his bow, and the other is full of painted arrows. Both of these cases are curiously wrought, and come from Babylon, as does also the targe, which is fitted to the left arm, and is proof only against arrows or the blows of a mace or sword. In the right hand, unless he prefers to keep it disengaged, is a light spear, which is generally painted green. Round his waist is girt a jewelled scimitar, while a mace of steel hangs from his saddle-bow. . . . The covering they wear on the head is made of the whitest and lightest cotton-cloth, in the middle of which rises a fluted peak of fine purple silk. It is a favorite fashion to ornament this head-dress with black plumes.[34]

Pages from the Hall of the Royal Bedchamber who had not held office passed at once into the Imperial Guard or were appointed to offices not lower in rank than the governorship of some important town and its out-lying district (*sandjaqbey*).[35] Pages who had held office automatically received the rank of pasha, and were appointed as vizirs, or lord admiral, or

to the four most considerable Governments, which are *Cairo, Aleppo, Damascus,* and *Buda,* or if none of these places be void, to be Beglerbegs of *Grecia,* or of *Natolia,* to be *Aga* [head] of the *Janizaries, Spaheeler Agasee* [head of the *Sipahis*] or General of the Horse, or to some small *Pashalicks* or Governments scattered in several places of the Empire.[36]

Under the Code of Laws of Muhammad II the first officer of the royal bedchamber and the sword-bearer could be promoted equally to the offices of head of the Boluks (*Boluk aghasi*), head-taster, and head gatekeeper of the Grand Seraglio (*qapuji bashi*).[37]   At a later period the sword-bearer was sometimes appointed directly to the grand vizirate, as were Ibrahim Pasha, Suleiman Agha in 1648, and Chorlu Ali Pasha, sword-bearer of Mustafa II, who was made grand vizir by Ahmed III, later becoming the husband of his daughter, Fatima Sultan.[38] The office of Janizary *Agha* is also said in the majority of instances to have been filled from the Hall of the Royal Bedchamber, for the reason that

it being an Office of great charge, it is thought necessary to be intrusted to one whose Education and Preferment hath made a Creature of the Court; which policy hath been the suppression of divers mutinies amongst the *Janizaries,* the discovery of their Combination, and an engagement to a stronger dependency on the favour of the Seraglio.[39]

If the sword-bearer or the master of the horse were dismissed with a pension (*cheraqluq*) instead of being appointed to active service upon leaving the Hall of the Royal Bedchamber, he received fifty *aqchas* a day, the remaining pages of the same hall under similar circumstances receiving thirty-five, those of the Hall of the Treasury from eighteen to twenty, and those of the Hall of the Commissariat sixteen.[40] Hafiz Elias Bey, a page in the Hall of the Treasury and author of *Jokes of the Palace School* (*Letaifi Enderun*), which covers the years 1812–1830, a period when the Palace School had already fallen into royal disfavor and neglect, gives the following rather naïve account of his own retirement:

Upon the return of the sultan from Rami, his farm beyond Eyyub, whither he had gone to review the troops, I asked my younger brother, the Chief Physican of the Sultan, and other friends, to secure my retirement and my appointment as scribe at the Suleimaniyeh Mosque, a position which had recently become vacant and for which there was a large number of applicants. After the fifth prayer on the third night of Ramazan I learned of my appointment to this post. First I knelt down and thanked Allah for so powerful a master who could work such miracles. Then, as was the custom at such times, I went to pay a visit to the head of our school, the Steward of the Treasury. When I knelt before him, he became very angry and said "Who made you a pensionner?" I was puzzled, and could only reply, "You know, Sir." His manner became milder and he finally said "Well, my son, so you are a pensionner! But I marvel how you will possibly be able to live on five thousand piastres a year. It was certainly no kindness on the part of your brother. May Allah help you. There is nothing more to be said or done!" I did not ask him what he really meant. I left him before daybreak, going to the house of the brother who had registered me at the palace during the reign of Selim III. He invited me to remain with him and advised me how to proceed with my affairs. May God grant him long life and prosperity! I had gone to the palace in 1227 A.H. [1812] when I was eleven years old, taking my own bed with me. I remained in the service of the Treasury nineteen years and I left in Ramazan 1246 A.H. [1830/1]. There were times when I could not bear the rebukes of my officers, but otherwise I have no criticism to make. I know that the judge and benefactor of us all is Allah!

Once having quitted the Grand Seraglio for the outside world a page was forbidden to enter its precincts, save only in the exceptional instance of his becoming grand vizir or mufti.[41]

CHAPTER VII

THE DECLINE OF THE PALACE SCHOOL

HOWEVER admirable the workings of the slave system of government during its best period, the effect of the exclusion of freeborn Turks from participation in the government was to retard the natural development of the Turkish people for several hundred years, "the Natural Turks," as old Knolles quaintly expresses it, "in the meantime, giving themselves wholly unto the Trade of Merchandise, and other their Mechanical Occupations; or else to the feeding of Cattel, their most ancient and natural Vocation, not intermeddling at all with matters of Government or State." [1] Once the decline of the empire was well under way in the seventeenth and eighteenth centuries, the effect of this exclusion upon the government itself was even more disastrous and far-reaching than upon the people:

The government was entirely divorced from all vital forces in the governed, so that the measure of development was the measure of decentralization. On the other hand the Turkish peasantry, still on the land, retained their racial health and strength of character, but remained peasants. Their sound stock never became available to revitalize the dying ruling class. So the power fell altogether out of Turkish hands into those of even lower racial types, as the follies and failures of the ruling Turks brought the government into less worthy hands. The Greek and Roumanian nobles who administered the empire for the Turks, as Hospodars in the provinces or as

Dragomans in the capital, threw the Turks over or were overthrown by them. The Armenian or Turkish officials of the middle class that took their place became in turn suspect and were replaced in turn under the Hamidian régime by Levantines, landless men, renegades, and rapscallions, and all the outlaws that haunt the borderland of East and West.[2]

Dissatisfaction with the slave form of government first began to make itself felt among the Janizaries, who may be likened during the period of Turkish decline to the Praetorian Guard of the Roman Empire. As early as 1568 Selim II, in response to their insistent demands, granted them the privilege of enrolling their sons in their own corps. In 1582 Murad III admitted aliens who were not slaves as "protégés" of the chief of the Janizaries.[3] By 1592 the majority are said to have been the sons of Janizaries. During the Turco-Persian war of 1594, the corps was finally thrown open to Turks and to Moslems in general. In the same year the Venetian *bailo*, Matteo Zane, wrote of the many and great changes that were taking place in the Turkish government: "One may reasonably hope, divine aid mediating, for some notable revolution within a short time, because the native Turks continue to sustain the greatest dissatisfaction, from seeing the government reposed in the renegades, who at a tender age for the most part, are taken into the seraglio of the king or of private citizens, and made Turks." [4] This comment is of particular interest when considered in connection with that of Guillaume Postel, already quoted above, to the effect that the Turks themselves believed that they were better and more faithfully served by a slave governing class. Apparently within the intervening sixty years, a marked change had taken place in the attitude of the Turkish people. By the end of the seventeenth century the slave system as a form of government had virtually broken down, although slaves continued to be employed in considerable numbers in the offices of the government until the final abolition of the royal slave household by Mahmud II.

There is no better proof of the vitality of the Palace School as an institution and of the effectiveness of its original organization than its slowness, even failure, to reflect the degenerating changes which were taking place in other political and social institutions of the Ottoman Empire. Forty years after the Janizaries had become an hereditary corps, entrance of Turks to the Palace School was still a privilege that was "effected but seldom and with very great difficulty." [5] Occasionally, upon the recommendation of the chief white eunuch, Turkish youths of great natural endowment from influential families were presented as slaves to the sultan, thereby becoming eligible for admission to the Palace School. It was considered worthy of remark that Muhammad Pasha, whom Ahmed I appointed grand vizir in 1615 to succeed Nasuh Pasha, was a Turk who, contrary to the usual custom, had been received into the *Saray* at an early age, and had been educated there.[6] Writing in 1675 of the difficulty experienced by Turks in obtaining admission into the Grand Seraglio, Tavernier says that the chief white eunuch "sticks not to admit into their number some natural Turks, such as may be recommendable upon the score of their good qualities and endowments. But that happens very seldom, and that not without the particular recommendation of the Prince, who would rather have all those Children to be Renegado Christians." During the eighteenth century and the first quarter of the nineteenth, when subject nationalities, particularly Greeks and even freeborn Turks, had come to be commonly employed in the government, the Palace School was still recruited from the slave markets, and graduates of the school received the rank of "pashas of three tails" and were appointed directly to the highest posts of the government. For a century and a half after the slave system of government of which it was a constituent part had ceased to prevail, the Palace School continued to recruit and train slaves for the government service, its graduates continuing to be appointed directly to some of the most important posts in the Empire.

It is not entirely clear when and where the Law of Tribute Children lapsed. It has long been popularly believed that it ceased to function after 1047 A.H. (1637/8), the last date when the levy is mentioned by Turkish historians as having taken place.[7] Pétis de La Croix, writing in his *État général de l'Empire Ottoman* in 1695, refers to the schools of Adrianople and Ibrahim Pasha as closed and gives the cessation of the draft as the reason for their closing.[8] On the other hand, evidence from the Registers of Payments to Military and Civil Officials (*Eulefe*), recently published in the *État militaire* of Djevad Bey, makes it certain that slave apprentices were employed in the Outer Service of the Grand Seraglio as late as 1164 A.H. (1750).[9] Further, tribute children were still being drawn from the Christian nations of the Caucasus as late as the Russo-Turkish War of 1768–1774, as is shown in Article xxiii of the famous Treaty of Kuchuk Kainardji (1774), in which the sultan renounced "solemnly and forever to exact tribute of children from the said Provinces of Georgia and Mingrelia."

That this agreement was borne out in practice is indicated by the following entry from the journal of the page Habesci, made in 1784, concerning the sources of slaves for the Palace School: "Prince Heraclius of Georgia has succeeded in freeing himself from this tribute only in the last war between the Turks and Russians, since which others have imitated him. Measures have also been taken against brigands, so that now Georgian slaves are very scarce." [10] It is suggested, as a probable explanation of what on the surface appears to be a contradiction, that the drafting of the tribute children ceased shortly after 1640 in the Balkans, but continued in the Caucasus for nearly a century and a half longer. As the supply of Christian slaves from this source declined and then failed altogether, the vacancies in the school were filled with slaves from other sources and, finally, with Turkish children levied directly by the sultan.[11]

One clear cause of the gradual decline of the Palace School is found within the school itself in the participation of the pages in the political intrigues of the seventeenth century. From the death of Suleiman the Magnificent in the middle of the sixteenth century until the reign of Mahmud II at the beginning of the nineteenth, the sultans were mostly figureheads, and the real power behind the throne was either the grand vizirate or the royal harem. The absence of a fixed custom or law of succession to the throne prior to the Constitution of

1876, which established the law of seniority,[12] introduced an element of chance in the succession which led to intense rivalry and intrigue among the mothers of the various princes and to the consequent formation of different factions which involved not only the harem but also the court and the army. The Janizaries and *Sipahis*, who were perpetually at strife with one another, supported one harem faction or another as best served their rival interests. In 1582 the pages, who naturally sympathized with the *Sipahis* and were made restless by their turbulence, attempted to join in a riot which occurred in the Hippodrome during the festivities attending the circumcision of Prince Muhammad, son of Murad III. The Janizaries had demanded as their customary present on this occasion one thousand *aqchas* a head, a sum which represented an increase of two *aqchas* a day, and in order to placate them the sultan had prolonged the ordinary forty days of feasting for another ten days, with the result that feeling between the two corps ran very high. A contemporary description of what followed is found in the state papers of the English ambassador, William Harborne:

Wednesday the 19th [July] very little of note took place at the Hippodrome, but at the twenty-third hour an incident of great importance occurred; the Subassi of Constantinople passing along a street saw a greek tavern with some Spahis and wished to attack it but a Spahi, one of the 500 newly come from the Serraglio begged the Subassi not to do so, but he despising the Spahi ordered the Janissaries of his guard to attack him, which being immediately done the Spahi receiving a blow on the head was killed. The Subassi then withdrew and the Janissaries seeing the multitude assembling fled, but being followed by the other Spahis and many people were captured. The Spahis having bound the Janissaries conducted them with the dead body to the Hippodrome in presence of the King, but on reaching there the Janissaries fell on them and the Spahis being reinforced by others they took to arms whereupon the chief Visir and the others with the [beylerbey] of Greece, came down from their boxes and went among the men shouting continuously and endeavouring to stop the riot and thereupon those of the scaffie (?), being the young men who wait on the King, having come down to the help of the Spahis the Basa came immediately to the door and persuaded them to go back saying the riot was over and caused the door to be closed. The Visir seeing that the new Aga of the Janissaries was taking the opportunity of encouraging the Janissaries causing more tumult than otherwise said some very . . . words to him saying that he was ill fulfilling his duty, and turning again to the people, by his efforts he separated them. Nevertheless 15 were killed, the majority being Spahis and many were wounded, and if these personages had not intervened and the matter taken in hand at once, certainly there would have been the worst slaughter between Spahis & Janissaries that has ever been witnessed and a catastrophe which would have remained in perpetual remembrance, but the might and the valour of the Bassa extinguished this severe fire, and the Subassi was imprisoned and it is said he will end badly.[13]

Again under Sultan Ibrahim the pages proved unruly. It was a long-established custom that at the accession of a sultan large numbers of pages who had completed their novitiate should be promoted from the auxiliary *sarays* to the reserve corps of the cavalry, a custom which was known as "the Deliverance" (*Chiqmeh*), but for some time it had been allowed to lapse. At the time of the tragic death of Osman II and of the accession of Sultan Ibrahim, the pages of Galata *Saray* and the Great and Small halls joined forces in reclaiming this privilege. When the chief white eunuch entered the Great Hall and threatened them with punishment, the pages forced him to withdraw and barricaded themselves within the hall. At a meeting of all the pages of the Grand Seraglio held later in the mosque of the Palace School it was decided to appeal to the *Sipahis* for support. The grand vizir intervening at this point, eighty of the leaders were expelled and the remainder were promised the desired promotion at the next *Bayram*.[14] This rebellious attitude on the part of the pages may have been one of the reasons why Sultan Ibrahim closed the schools of Adrianople and Ibrahim Pasha.

Once more, at the accession of Muhammad IV (1648), the pages of Galata Saray and of the Great and Small halls, together with a thousand *Sipahis* who had recently been dismissed by the grand vizir, assembled in the Hippodrome to demand their own promotions and the execution of those who had taken part in the deposition and death of Ibrahim, and again were successful in obtaining their demands. These revolts resulted in a decree against the custom of a universal "Deliverance," and in the substitution of promotions from time to time on the occasion of the appointment of a *beylerbey* or pasha. At such a time the sultan would accord the new official a fitting number of pages for his suite from the upper halls, the vacancies thus created being filled from the lower halls and these in turn from the auxiliary schools.[15]

In the struggle between the grandmother of Muhammad IV, Kiusem or Mahpeyker Sultan, and his mother, Turkhan Sultan, for the control of the government during the minority of the young sultan, the dowager queen-mother was supported by the sword-bearer, the majority of the black eunuchs, and the Janizaries, while the party of the young queen-mother consisted of the grand vizir, Siavush Pasha, the white eunuchs under the leadership of the chief black eunuch, Suleiman Agha, and the pages of the Grand Seraglio. Upon the second of September, 1651, the demands of the Janizaries for the banishment into Egypt of three of the white eunuchs who were partisans of Turkhan Sultan not having been granted, the dowager queen-mother, Mahpeyker Sultan, commanded the head gardener to open several of the postern gates of the Grand Seraglio, in order that the Janizaries might enter during the night and take possession of the palace. In the struggle which ensued between them and the palace faction the pages played a prominent part, two of the pages of the Great Hall actually strangling the old dowager and robbing the body of the rich jewels which she was accustomed to wear. Although the death of his grandmother in all probability saved Muhammad IV his throne, he is said to have curtailed the possibility of further rebellion on the part of the pages by closing the Great and Small halls. In 1788 it was remarked by d'Ohsson, as has already been said above, that the sum total of the royal pages was no more than six hundred, two hundred in Galata *Saray* and four hundred in the Grand Seraglio, and that only the four upper schools of the Grand Seraglio were in existence.[16]

With the sweeping-away of antiquated institutions and the introduction of western culture, especially of western education, by Mahmud II, it was inevitable that the system of palace education as a remnant of the slave system of government should fall under the royal ban. As an indication of the neglect and poverty into which the remaining schools were consciously allowed to fall during the first part of the reign, even while they still remained officially state schools, may be quoted the realistic picture of Galata *Saray* given by Hafiz Elias Bey upon the occasion of a royal visit in the year 1235 A.H. (1819/20):

The sultan, accompanied by his bodyguard and the diplomatic corps, arrived at Galata Saray and was received by the pages arrayed in very ragged *qaftans* of many colors and headdresses which were made of cardboard covered with red cloth, strongly resembling nightcaps. When they were commanded to play *chalik chomaq*, they entreated to be excused on the plea that they were not so well trained as the pages of the Grand Seraglio, whom the sultan was accustomed to see play this game. Their request having been refused, the game was begun, but when shortly some of the players showed so great lack of skill as to strike each other, the sultan abruptly ordered them to stop. It was the usual custom, following this game, for the sword-bearer to throw gold coins to the players, but upon this occasion, inasmuch as it was feared that the coins might strike the flesh of the players which their rags left bare, the sum of about two and a half liras was handed to each of them. The ambassadors presented many baskets of candy to Sultan Mahmud, which pleased him and which he ordered to be sent to the women of the royal harem. So great a quantity of this candy was there that it required twenty old slaves to transport it. The sultan on his part commanded the head gardener to distribute gifts of money to the ambassadors. Before taking his leave the sultan requested the musicians of Galata *Saray* to present themselves before the royal kiushk and to play and sing for him. The sultan, who was himself an excellent musician and composer, rewarded each musician individually. Six senior students were promoted at this time to the three halls of the Grand Seraglio.[17]

Further loss of prestige is also seen in the fact that the pages now no longer demanded to leave the palace, or, in the rare event of their doing so, received only petty appointments, with the exception of the officers of the royal bedchamber, who were still appointed directly to the most eminent posts of the Empire.[18]

The account given by Hafiz Elias Bey of the sweeping reforms which the new sword-bearer, Devletlu (His Excellency) Ali Agha Hazretleri, found it necessary to make at the time of his appointment about the year 1237 A.H. (1821/2) indicates that the organization of the Palace School had at last broken down. The pages of the royal bedchamber were now in the habit of leaving the palace without permission and of remaining away for an indeterminate time, even of marrying and maintaining homes in the city. Devletlu Ali Agha searched out the guilty pages one by one and "retired them with pensions" (*timareh chikmak*), a very polite phrase which was applied only to the service of the royal palace and which meant literally "to give one the leisure to take care of one's self." The master of the wardrobe was retired with a pension of one hundred piastres a month, a disciplinary measure which inspired the pages with great awe. Eleven others who had seen about twenty-five years of service in the palace, and who were very loath to leave, received pensions of fifty piastres a month. Henceforth permission to leave the palace for only one day at a time was given to the pages. Other old laws and regulations were revived by the sword-bearer and strictly enforced; in especial, the entire student body was required to pray for the sultan five times a day.[19]

In 1826 Mahmud II destroyed the Janizaries and began to build a new army along European lines. With the inauguration of this military reform, the pages, of whom there were still some four or five hundred in the Grand Seraglio, eagerly sought the privilege of the new training. The new titles and decorations once received, however, their enthusiasm quickly cooled. During one of the sultan's absences at the suburb of Therapia it is related that the pages were neglectful of their drill and other duties, and that the sword-bearer, who was in charge of the discipline of the school and had only the steward of the treasury to assist him, was unable to bring order into the situation. Upon his return to Stambul, Sultan Mahmud took a drastic step which can scarcely be regarded as other than the formal disestablishment of the Palace School as a state institution. He revoked the recent decorations and dismissed the entire student body.[20] Henceforth the Palace School of the Grand Seraglio continued an attenuated existence as a training school for court functionaries and palace domestics until the establishment of the Turkish Republic in 1922, when it ceased to function after a continuous existence of more than four hundred and fifty years.

Of the nine schools which comprehended the palace system of education, the Galata *Saray* alone has survived the changing times. In 1828 Sultan Mahmud rebuilt it almost entirely and added a school of medicine, intending to have taught there, in addition to the medical sciences, French, Latin, German, geography, astronomy, and so on; but at the time of his death the reforms were only partially inaugurated, and after the accession of his son, Sultan Abd ul-Mejid, they were not continued.[21] In 1868 it was reorganized under French direction and still exists today, the best of the Turkish *lycées* and of the preparatory schools for Istanbul University. As the sole survivor of the old palace system of education, it might appropriately be chosen to carry on the once great traditions of the Palace School in evolving, in connection with the university, a school of public administration or civil service for the flourishing Turkish Republic.

With the conversion of the Grand Seraglio into a national museum in 1924 the pages of the royal bedchamber were transformed into "Curators of the Holy Relics." One of these, Ferid Bey, the senior officer, who, in 1928, was said to have been in the palace service for more than sixty-five years and who was regarded with singular reverence on account of his piety, was more than one hundred years old. The other thirty-odd elderly pages remaining from the Inner Service served as secretaries and attendants of the museum. Nine old white eunuchs acted as gatekeepers at the great Central Gate, which is the entrance to the museum today.

Sic transit gloria mundi!

NOTES

NOTES

FOREWORD

1. Paolo Giovio, *L'Histoire des empereurs de Turquie* (Paris, 1538), p. I iiii.

2. Ottaviano Bon, *Il serraglio del gransignore* (1608), ed. G. Berchet (Venice, 1865), p. 36; Robert Withers, "Description of the Grant Seigneur's Seraglio or Turkish Emperor's Court," in John Greaves, *Miscellaneous Tracts, Letters, Poems* (London, 1736–37), II, 668–669.

3. Michel Baudier, *Histoire géneralle du serrail, et de la cour du Grand Seigneur, Empereur des Turcs* (Paris, 1624), preface, pp. 114, 119.

4. Blaise de Vigenère, *Illustrations de Blaise de Vigenère Bourbonnois sur l'histoire de Chalcondile, Athénien*. A continuation of Chalcondyles, *Histoire de la décadence de l'empire grec et établissement de celuy des Turcs . . . De la traduction de B(laise) de Vigenère Bourbonnois* (Rouen, 1660), p. 53.

5. Sir Paul Rycaut, *The Present State of the Ottoman Empire, containing the Maxims of the Turkish Politie . . . and a particular Description of the Seraglio* (London, 1670), p. 42, hereafter referred to as *Present State*.

6. Albert Bobovi, "Serai enderum [*sic*] cioè," trans. anonymously under the title "Mémoires sur les Turcs." Dated Constantinople, November 10, 1666 (Count Paul Riant Collection, Harvard University MS, Ott. 3030.4), fol. 8; referred to hereafter as "Harvard MS." The folios of this MS are numbered only in the first part.

7. Tayyar Zadeh Mehmed Ata, *Tarikh-i Ata* (5 vols., Constantinople, 1874–76), II, 1–3. The *Tarikh-i Ata* is the most important study of the Palace School which has as yet been made in Turkish. The father and grandfather and Ata Bey himself, three generations which spanned the five reigns from Selim III to Sultan Abd ul-Aziz, all were court functionaries trained in the Grand Seraglio during the late period when the Palace School was on the verge of disestablishment as a state institution, but while it was still impossible to make intimate disclosures concerning the palace life. The first volume covers the history of the school from its beginning until the reign of Suleiman. The second and third volumes contain biographical sketches of the more important graduates and students of the school. The two remaining volumes are an anthology of the writings (more especially the verse) of the pages, of other members of the court and of the sultans. As Ata Bey seldom documents his statements and has not always weighed his evidence carefully, the work must be used with some caution.

8. *Ibid.*, I, 40 ff.; III, 95.

9. J(oseph Freiherr) von Hammer-Purgstall, *Des osmanischen Reichs Staatsverfassung und Staatsverwaltung* (Vienna, 1815), II, 8–32. It is probable that in this interpretation of the status of pages von Hammer was following the early European meaning of the term, which in France, until the reigns of Charles VI and Charles VII, was applied only to *viles personnes*, such as *garçons de pieds*, etc. (Claude Fauchet, 1530–1601, as quoted by Littré in *Encyclopaedia Britannica*, 13th ed.)

10. Mehmed Refik Bey, "Organization of the Palace School at the time of Muhammad II," *Edebiyat-i Osmaniyeh Mejmuasi*, Feb. 4, 1913, p. 274.

11. Leopold von Ranke, *The Ottoman and Spanish Empires in the Sixteenth and Seventeenth Centuries*, trans. W. H. Kelly (London, 1843), p. 15.

CHAPTER I

1. The *medreseh* was a relatively late development in Islamic education. The earliest stage was that of the regular academies, or mosque schools, which existed from the time of the *Tabi's* (those who had known the Companions of the Prophet). Here were taught the Koran, Traditions, Arabic, and the "religious sciences" relating to the Koran. Somewhat later there developed the private schools in which the house of a learned man was made the center of advanced study or of instruction in those subjects which could not be obtained in the mosque schools, especially the quadrivium, and training of a technical nature to supplement the apprenticeship system. These private schools were usually small, but very numerous. The second stage was marked by the innovation of centers of translation (*dar al-hikmah*, house of wisdom) which were established for the purpose of translating ancient Greek learning into Arabic. Because of the persecution of scholars in the fifth and sixth centuries, the center of Hellenistic learning had passed from Constantinople to Syria, Mesopotamia, and Persia, particularly to the schools at Edessa, Nisibis, and Jundeshapur. When Islam was expanded to include these lands, it was inevitable that it should be, as had been Christianity before it, "reclothed in Greek thought"; and thus began the Golden Age of Arabic translation of medical literature, mathematics, and other sciences, the works of Aristotle and Neoplatonic treatises, which lasted from about 750 to 900 A.D. The first important *dar al-hikmah* was the *Bayt al-Hikmah*, founded in Baghdad in 198–202 A.H. (813/4–817/8 A.D.) by the Abbasid Caliph, al-Mamun, which, from a library for translation with a notable collection of manuscripts and many competent specialists to translate them, became also a higher institution of learning, and the prototype of numerous later foundations of the same kind. Because of the inherently

close connection between *Shiah* mysticism and Greek metaphysics, these institutions in Fatimid countries took on a definitely *Shiah* character and were made centers of *Shiah* propaganda. The *Dar al-Hikmah* of the Fatimid rulers in Cairo, with its library of six thousand five hundred volumes, where the entire quadrivium and other sciences were taught, is a notable illustration. It was mainly to combat *Shiah* propaganda, as has been said above, that the orthodox *Sunnis* originated the *medreseh*, which marks the third and last stage of Moslem higher education in the Middle Ages. (Ibn Khallikan, *Biographical Dictionary*, trans. MacGuckin de Slane, London, 1842, vol. I, Introduction, pp. xxvii–xxxii; Ernest Dietz, "The Mosque as an Education Centre," *Encyclopaedia of Islam*, Leyden, 1936, III, 350 ff.; Philip K. Hitti, *History of the Arabs*, London, 1937, chaps. XXVIII, XL; Asad Talas, *L'Enseignement chez les Arabes: La Madrasa Nizamiyya et son histoire*, Paris, 1939, pp. 1, 17–19.)

2. The series of lapses and renewals which were so characteristic of the University of Constantinople make it particularly difficult to reconstruct its history. Constantine the Great is said to have established a school in the Great Palace with "nearly twenty professors," which somewhat later, as it dwindled in numbers, was moved to less pretentious quarters. The university of Theodosius II, whom Professor Bury credits with having been the founder of the University of Constantinople in 425 A.D., had thirty-one professors, including ten professors and five *rhetors* (lectors) of Greek literature and grammar, and ten professors and three lectors of Latin literature and grammar, a proportion which is said to have marked "a stage in the official Graecisation of the eastern half of the Roman Empire" (J. B. Bury, *History of the Later Roman Empire*, London, 1923, I, 231–232). Under the Edict of March 15 of the same year, it was decreed that university professors must hold government licences and that at the end of twenty years of service they should receive the title of "Counts of the First Rank." In spite of the efforts of the Emperor Justinian, which are seen in the increase in the number of professorships to thirty-three and the special emphasis put upon juridical studies, the university is said to have entered upon a decline and not to have been mentioned after the close of his reign (F. Schemmel, *Die Hochschule von Konstantinopel vom 9–12 Jahrhundert*, Berlin, 1912, pp. 4–7). The so-called "University of the Octagon," which Leo III has been accused of having caused to be destroyed by fire along with its entire personnel because he could not convert them to his particular heresy, seems to have been, not the Imperial University, but a small school of the "oecumenical," or perhaps patriarchal, type, in which instruction was given in both secular and religious subjects (F. Fuchs, "Die höheren Schulen von Konstantinopel im Mittelalter," *Byzantinisches Archiv*, no. 8, Berlin, 1926, pp. 10, 11; Schemmel, *op.*

cit., pp. 9–10). The university was revived in the Palace of the Magnaura in 863 by Caesar Bardas, who ruled in the name of his nephew, Michael III (839–867). It was placed under the direction of Leo of Thessalonica, "one of the greatest minds of the ninth century," who also held the chair of philosophy. Other subjects taught were Greek literature, mathematics, and astronomy. Although state-supported, there is no certainty that it trained members of the bureaucracy, but the high degree of the culture of the period and the large number of scholars, in particular Photius, who has been sometimes called "the greatest scholar of the Middle Ages," would suggest that such may have been the case (*Cambridge Mediaeval History*, IV, 43–48; J. M. Hussey, *Church and Learning in the Byzantine Empire, 867–1185*, London, 1937, pp. 23-25; A. Andréades, "Le Recrutement des fonctionnaires et les universités dans l'empire byzantin," *Mélanges de droit roman dédiés à Georges Cornil*, Paris, 1926, pp. 17–40). Following the death of its founder, the university lapsed during the reigns of Basil I (867–886) and Leo VI (886–912). It was revived for the second time by Constantine Porphyrogenitus (912–959), who was interested in all branches of knowledge and in the arts, a patron of every kind of writing, and himself the author of "the most monumental, and certainly the most interesting, historical works of the tenth century" . . . in particular of *Excerpta de Legationibus*, "which had for its chief object the formation of high functionaries." His unusual interest in the university was manifested in the policies of free instruction and of close personal relations with the student body which he initiated. Students who completed the university course were appointed to high positions in the judiciary, treasury, and church (Hussey, *op. cit.*, pp. 24, 25, 28, 29; Andréades, *op. cit.*, p. 22). From the death of Constantine Porphyrogenitus until the revival of the university by Constantine Monomachus in 1045 there was no higher instruction. This third revival is said to have been "inspired by the disastrous effect which the neglect of legal studies had had on the civil government" and the "urgent public need for a school of law." Its main innovation was, as has been said above, the thorough democratization of the bureaucracy. There were two faculties of law and of philosophy. The constitution of the faculty of law, which is still extant, affords unusual wealth of detail. Xiphilinus, a lawyer famed for his knowledge of case law, who was appointed principal and professor of the faculty of law (*Nomophylax*) by the emperor, was paid by him and was removable by him only. He counted among the senators of highest rank. His seat was next to that of the High Judge, and he alone accompanied the judge in audience with the emperor. The diploma of the university, or state diploma, was necessary for the exercise of the offices of advocate and notary and for eligibility to high administrative office, with the result that the university had almost a monopoly of the legal training of the Empire (Hussey, *op. cit.*, pp. 52–58). Psellus, Neo-platonist and "the complete antithesis of the ecclesiastical ideals of the Greek Church," who was the center of the intellectual life of Constantinople and the most prominent figure in the revival of learning of the eleventh century, was principal and professor of the faculty of philosophy. His two friends, Nicetas of Byzantium and John Mauropos, occupied respectively the subordi-nate chairs of grammar and rhetoric. The elementary course (grammar, rhetoric, and dialectic) and the more advanced course (arithmetic, geometry, astronomy, and music) corresponded to the Trivium and Quadrivium of the West. The culminating point, "the goal of a long and varied course," was philosophy, especially the works of Plato and the *Logic* of Aristotle, which Psellus alone appears to have taught (Hussey, *op. cit.*, pp. 59–88; Andréades, *op. cit.*, pp. 28–30). From this stage on, authorities differ, some holding that the university may not have outlived Constantine Monomachus, who died in 1054, and that scholarship and literature were at their lowest ebb during the last decades before the fall of Constantinople (Hussey, *op. cit.*, p. 71; Andréades, *op. cit.*, pp. 31–32; S. Panaretoff, *Near Eastern Affairs and Con-ditions*, New York, 1922, pp. 66–67, 70); while, on the other hand, Professor A. A. Vasiliev is of the opinion that the schools in Constantinople continued "to flourish during the fourteenth and fifteenth centuries as in the most brilliant past" (*History of the Byzantine Empire*, 2 vols., Madison, 1928–29, I, 443–446). Schemmel in particular shares this view and produces the fol-lowing data in support of the theory that the university lingered on until the fall of Constantinople. Dating from the accession of Alexis Comnenus (1048–1118), the university, which about this time was transferred to the Orphanage of Alexis, continued for at least two generations, Psellus being succeeded by one of his pupils, who in turn was succeeded by Theodorus of Smyrna, after whom the professorship of philosophy remained vacant for about fifty years. Seemingly as the effect of the Latin conquest of Constanti-nople, which is said to have destroyed everything of value which had been accomplished in the preceding three hundred years, the financial sufferings of the faculty became so great that the university was closed by the gram-marian Hyrtakenos, who appears to have been in charge at the time. About 1315, while on a visit to Constantinople, the lector Theodulos of Thessalonica made the rounds of the metropolitan schools and wrote with special pleasure of the instruction at the university. It is said to have been about this time that Italians first began to come to Constantinople to learn Greek, as they formerly had gone to Athens, and the vogue increased until it was said that "no one was educated who had not studied there." Manuel Chrysolas (1355–1415), who was "very skilled in Greek," is thought to have been active in the university before his departure for Italy. The last famous teacher in the university is said to have been Johannes Argyropulos, who was in Constantinople until 1441, when he was called to Padua. Having returned to his homeland in 1445, he sought refuge in Rome with the fall of Constantinople in 1453 (Schemmel, "Die Schulen von Konstantinopel vom 12–15 Jahrhundert," *Philologischen Wochenschrift*, 1925, pp. 235–239; Fuchs, *op. cit.*, p. 57).

3. The events leading to the founding of the *Nizamiyeh* are described by Max von Berchem as follows: "The *madrasah* was the creation of Nizam ul-Mulk. . . . His antecedents, his early environment and education, and later his public career, all explain his part in this matter. His father was employed in Tus, one of the Sunnite strongholds in Khorasan, the country even of al-Ghazzali. From his early youth Nizam ul-Mulk consecrated himself to religious studies and his brother Abdullah became a distinguished jurist. Entered into political life, Nizam ul-Mulk naturally allied himself with the Sunnite party of reform. About the middle of the fifth century (eleventh century A.D.) he founded a *madrasah* at Nishapur for the celebrated jurist Djuwaini. Several years later, he erected a second (the *Nizamiyeh*) at Baghdad for the famous al-Shirazi, then at the apogee of his popularity." (*Matériaux pour un Corpus inscriptorum arabicum: Mémoires publiées par les membres de la Mission archéologique française au Caire*, Paris, 1903, vol. XIX, fascicule III, p. 260.)

4. Nizam ul-Mulk, *Siasset Nameh: Traité de gouvernement* (1091/2 A.D.), trans. Charles Schefer (Paris, 1897), p. 138. Schefer, who is said by V. V. Bartold not to be always accurate, gives *chavush* (sergeant) as the equivalent of *ghulam*, but Bartold translates it consistently as slave (*Turkestan down to the Mongol Invasion*, London, 1928, pp. 227–228).

5. An extremely interesting, and apparently unique, description of Turkish characteristics and the value of Turkish slave regiments to the Abbasid caliphate is given by Jahiz of Basra, 150–255 A.H. (767–868 A.D.), a famous historian and theologian who occupied an eminent position at the Abbasid court, in a treatise "Exploits of the Turks and the Army of the Khalifate in General," trans. C. R. Harley Walker, *Journal of the Royal Asiatic Society of Great Britain and Ireland*, 1915, II, 631–697, cited by Bartold, *op. cit.*, p. 197.

6. Bartold, *op. cit.*, pp. 226–228, 309.

7. For description of a teaching licence in the fourteenth century, see Ibn Batuta, *Voyages*, trans. C. Defrémery and Dr. R. B. Sanguinetti (Paris, 1859–79), I, 248–250.

8. Von Berchem, *op. cit.*, p. 261. The tomb of Humayun in the vicinity of New Delhi, as also the tombs of Timur and of such of his descendants as ruled in Samarcand, had *medresehs* attached to them (N. N. Law, *Promotion of Learning in India during Muhammadan Rule*, London & New York, 1916, p. 69).

9. Ibn Khallikan, *op. cit.*, vol. I, Introduction, p. xxxi.

10. *Medresehs* were founded in Cairo in 395 A.H. (1004/5 A.D.) and 400 A.H. (1009/10 A.D.), and a third in Baghdad in 416 A.H. (1025/6 A.D.). In the following half-century in Nishapur (Khorasan), a city which had been previously noted for its private schools, there were four especially famous *medresehs*, the fourth of which was the first of the numerous *medresehs* founded by Nizam ul-Mulk (Ernest Dietz, "Origin and Spread of the Madrasa," *Encyclopaedia of Islam*, III, 350 ff.; Ibn Khallikan, *op. cit.*, vol. I, Introduction, pp. xxvii–xxxii, 117).

11. A paraphrase of Von Berchem, *op. cit.*, pp. 260–263; Ernest Dietz, "Nizam ul-Mulk," *Encyclopaedia of Islam*, III, 350–354.

12. Ibn Khallikan, *op. cit.*, vol. I, Introduction, p. xxxii; Asad Talas, who gives no more than one and a half pages to the curriculum of the Nizamiyah (*op. cit.*, pp. 37–38), does not mention a separate section in preparation for public administration, but in his list of its more famous students he includes several secretaries to princes and vizirs; diplomats and confidential envoys to the caliphs; one inspector of the *Wakf* (Ministry of Pious Foundation); one district administrator; historians; grammarians; calligraphers; and numerous men of letters, especially poets, among them the celebrated Saadi of Shiraz (pp. 86, 88, 89, 91, 95–98).

13. Julian Ribera y Tarrago, *La enseñanza entre los Musulmanes españoles* (Cordova, 1925), p. 243, n; *Origin de colegio Nidami de Baghdad* (Zaragoza, 1914), pp. 361–362.

14. Law, *op. cit.*, pp. 17–18, 50–55, 63, 73–74, 139–165.

15. Hitti, *op. cit.*, p. 299; G. Le Strange, *Baghdad during the Abbasid Caliphate* (London, 1924), p. 411.

16. The question has been recently raised whether the Turks were not perhaps more vitally influenced by Byzantine culture rather than by Islam, from which they took their faith and social system. In a course of lectures given at the Sorbonne in the autumn of 1931, Professor Nicholas Jorga maintained the thesis that the Ottoman Empire was in fact the continuation of the Byzantine Empire; and that the slave system of government, in conception and in spirit, if not in actual fact, has been evident in the relationship of the Byzantine emperor to the official class and to the dependencies of the Empire (such as Venice and other Italian states): "pour employer le terme même qui a passé du grec byzantin dans le langage des diplômes latins, ce sont des 'duli imperatoris,' ce sont ses 'esclaves.'" (N. Jorga, *Deux siècles d'histoire de Venise*, Bucharest, 1932, pp. 2, 16, 20–21; Le Vte. de La Jonquière, *Histoire de l'empire ottoman depuis les origines jusqu'à nos jours*, Paris, 1914, I, 100–101, 128.)

17. For further discussion of the sultan's quota of prisoners of war, see Notes, Chap. III, n. 13, below.

18. J. H. Kramers, "Murad II," *Encyclopaedia of Islam*, III, 728-729; IV, 943 f.

19. Johann Schiltberger, *Bondage and Travels of Johann Schiltberger, a Native of Bavaria, in Europe, Asia, Africa* (1396-1427), trans. J. B. Telfert and P. Brun (London, 1879), Introduction, p. 5.

20. The custom of educating a certain number of the palace pages with the royal princes was still in force during the reign of Mustafa IV (1754–1794), when Cherkess (Circassian) Khalil Efendi, son of the nurse of Hibeteh-ullah Sultan, daughter of the sultan, was reared in the royal harem with the young Prince Selim, the former being educated in the Hall of the Treasury and thereafter serving as the steward of the Treasury for thirteen years (Hafiz Elias Bey, *Letai'fi Enderun* [*Jokes of the Palace School*], Constantinople, 1859). The events of the late period which this journal chronicles are not of major importance for the history of the Palace School, but the description of the daily life, customs, etc., which varied little during the centuries, is valuable as a mirror of better days.

21. J. de Hammer, *Histoire de l'empire ottoman*, trans. from the German by J. J. Hellert, 18 vols. and atlas (Paris, 1835–41), III, 326, hereafter referred to as *Histoire*; E. J. W. Gibb, *A History of Ottoman Poetry* (London, 1900–1909), I, 229; II, 18, 40. For a complete list of the savants attached to the court of Muhammad and his son Bayazid, see *Histoire*, III, 439, n. xxiii. For the list of the preceptors of the sultans, see Hajji Halifa, *Chronologia historica* (Venice, 1697), pp. 195 f.

22. Ali Efendi, *Kunh al-Akhbar; Histoire*, III, 18.

23. A. Cambini, *Two very Notable Commentaries* (London, 1562), *Second Commentary*, pp. 1-2; T. Pelletier, *Histoire des ottomans* (Paris, 1600), pp. 117-118. A. Gegaj, who has written the most recent history of Albania during the period of Scanderbey, adds nothing new concerning his education. His statement that Scanderbey entered the Janizary corps and served with it in Asia Minor seems improbable, inasmuch as the members of this corps do not appear to have been educated at court even in the early period, and the title of *sandjak-bey*, which was conferred upon him at this time, was that of a high officer of the cavalry or of a governor of a *sandjak*, a subdivision of a province (*L'Albanie et l'invasion turque au XVᵉ siècle*, Louvain, 1937, pp..42–44).

24. *Histoire*, III, 329.

25. Pelletier, *op. cit.*, p. 106; Barthélémy d'Herbelot, *La Bibliothèque orientale* (Paris, 1697), p. 615; Namiq Kemal Bey, *Evraqi Perishan* (Constantinople, 1872/3), pp. 130 ff.

26. G. de St. Guillet, *Histoire du règne de Mahomet II* (Paris, 1601), I, 13; Pelletier, *op. cit.*, p. 106. Larousse defines the *masse d'armes* as an "arme

formée d'un manche assez court, que surmonte une tête de metal, souvent garnie de pointes."

27. *Histoire*, II, 394–395.

28. Saad ad-Din (Khojah Efendi), *Chronica dell'origine, e progressi della casa ottomana*, trans. V. Brattuti (pt. I, Vienna, 1649; pt. II, Madrid, 1652).

29. *Annales sultanorum Othmanidarum* (Frankfort, 1588), p. 582.27 (1453 A.D.).

30. *Histoire*, III, 300, 326, 330–332, 438, n. xxii; Guillet, *op. cit.*, I, 13–19.

31. *Histoire*, III, 327–329; *Tarikh-i Ata*, I, 40.

32. *Tarikh-i Ata*, I, 5.

33. Gibb, *op. cit.*, II, 22 f.

34. Gio(vanni) Maria Angiolello, *Historia turchesca di Gio Angiolello schiavo et altri schiavi dall'anno 1429 sui 1513* (Bibl. Nat., fonds ital., 1238), fols. 27–28, 52.

35. *Tarikh-i Ata*, I, 40.

36. Namiq Kemal Bey, *op. cit.*, says also that examples of letters and treaties written by these Greek scribes are to be found in the Imperial Library in Vienna.

37. Critobule d'Imbros (Critoboulus), "Vie de Mahomet II (1453–1467)," *Monum. Hung. Hist. Script. XXI*, deuxième partie (Budapest, 187–?), p. 291.

38. *Ibid.*, pp. 346–348.

39. Angiolello, *op. cit.*, fols. 48–50, 502; L. Thuasne, *Gentile Bellini et Sultan Mohammed II* (Paris, 1888), pp. vi, 2, 10–11, 15–16, 19, 68–70; D. Adolf Deissmann, *Forschungen und Funden im Serai* (Berlin and Leipzig, 1933), pp. 27, 105–111.

40. "Qanun-name-yi Al-i Osman Suret-i Khatt-i Humayun-u Sultan Muhammad Khan," ed. Mehmed Arif Bey, *Tarikh-i Osmani Enjumeni Mejmuasi*, nos. 13, 14, 1330 A.H. (April, June, 1912). At the time of Bayazid II, the novices are said to have received thirty-one *aqchas* per day (*Tarikh-i Ata*, I, p. 67).

41. *Tarikh-i Ata*, I, 39, 41.

42. *Ibid.*, I, 7, 39–41; Ahmed Rasim, *Resimli ve Kharitali Osmanli Tarikh-i* (Constantinople, 1910).

43. For a discussion of the plan of Muhammad's palace, see Barnette Miller, *Beyond the Sublime Porte* (New Haven: Yale Press, 1931), pp. 38–39.

44. Evliya Efendi (Evliya Chelebi), *Narrative of Travels in Europe, Asia, and Africa in the Seventeenth Century*, trans. from the Turkish by the Ritter Joseph von Hammer (2 vols., London, 1834), I, 49, hereafter referred to as *Narrative of Travels; Tarikh-i Ata*, I, 59.

45. The Turkish historian Ali Efendi, *op. cit.*, who wrote about 1597, gives the number of pages in the Palace School during the reign of Muham-

mad II as 282: 32 in the Hall of the Royal Bedchamber, 60 each in the Hall of the Treasury and the Small Hall, 30 in the Hall of the Commissariat, and 100 in the Great Hall. With the exception of the pages of the royal bedchamber, which he puts at the traditional number of 40, Mehmed Refiq Bey's figures are the same as those of Ali Efendi (*Edebiyat-i Osmaniyeh Mejmuasi*, Feb. 4, 1913). Theodoros Spanduginos, who wrote in 1519, puts the sum total at 300 (Theodore Spandouyn Cantacasin, *Petit Traicté de l'origine des Turcqz* (1519), ed. Charles Schefer, Paris, 1896, p. 59). Menavino mentions 15 "valets" of the royal bedchamber, 35 of the "wardrobe," and 80–100 of the New Hall; but he omits the numbers of the halls of the Treasury and Commissariat (Gio[vanni] Antonio Menavino, *I costumi, et la vita de Turchi* [Florence, 1551], pp. 91–95, first published under the title, *Trattato di costumi et vita de Turchi*, Rome, 1548). Menavino was the scion of a wealthy Genoese family of Voltri. At the age of twelve, in the course of a voyage which he and his father were making to Venetia, their convoy was attacked off the coast of Corsica by Barbary corsairs, and, after a spectacular engagement, the two were taken prisoners and carried to Anatolia to be sold into slavery. The father shortly died. Giovanni, who was unusually clever and well instructed for his years, was presented to Bayazid II and became a page in the Grand Seraglio. Although he remained there for nearly a decade, he never grew reconciled to the separation from his family, nor to expatriation from "our Italy," as he lovingly calls the land of his birth. Taken by Sultan Selim on his Persian campaign, he contrived to escape and to return to Genoa. In his *Trattato di costumi et vita de Turchi* he devotes fifteen octavo pages to a narrative of his capture, his reception by Sultan Bayazid and his admission to the Palace School, and to the training which he received in its several different halls. It was the first account of the Palace School to be published.

46. Angiolello, *op. cit.*, fols. 50–51.

47. "Qanun-name-yi . . . Sultan Muhammad Khan," *Tarikh-i Osmani Enjumeni Mejmuasi*, no. III, supplement 13.

48. *Ibid.*

49. Menavino, *op. cit.*, pp. 91–95, 102–103; Mehmed Refiq Bey, *Edebiyat-i Osmaniyeh Mejmuasi*, Feb. 4, 1913. Von Hammer, who probably follows Ali Efendi in the matter, says that the Hall of the Royal Bedchamber and the Great and Small halls existed at the time of Muhammad II. Although he mentions the heads of the Treasury and Commissariat and says that the chief duty of the white eunuchs was the care of the pages, he does not specifically mention either the Hall of the Treasury or the Hall of the Commissariat (*Histoire*, III, 318).

50. Navagero, *Relazione*, in Eugenio Alberi, *Relazione degli ambasciatori Veneti al Senato* (Florence, 1839–63), ser. III, vol. I, pp. 42–45, hereafter referred to as *Relazione*.

51. Angiolello, *op. cit.*, fol. 49.

52. Elias Habesci, *État actuel de l'empire ottoman* . . . *avec une description particulière de la cour et du serail du Grand Seigneur* (1784), trans. M. Fontanelle (Paris, 1792), I, 157–187, 289.

53. *Histoire*, X, 192.

54. *Palais de Topkapou* (Constantinople, 1925), pp. 23–24. On the other hand, von Hammer says it was founded by Murad IV during the Erivan campaign (*Staatsverwaltung*, p. 28).

CHAPTER II

1. *I costumi, et i modi particolari de la vita de Turchi* (Rome, 1545), cap. XIII.

2. *Antiquities of Constantinople*, trans. John Ball (London, 1729), p. 204.

3. Jean Baptiste Tavernier, *Nouvelle Relation de l'Intérieur du serrail du Grand Seigneur* (Paris, 1675). Tavernier devotes two chapters of his *Nouvelle Relation* to the Palace School. He includes its organization and training, "the Great Charges and Dignitaries of the Empire" to which its students were eligible, and the buildings of the third court. Although gleaned at second hand from two renegade officials of the Palace School, this account is as vivid and detailed as a stenographic report. Unless otherwise specified, the edition herein referred to is the translation by J. P(hillips), *The Six Voyages* . . . *through Persia into Turky and the East Indies, finished in the year 1670* . . . *together with a New Relation of the Present Grand Seignor's Seraglio* (London, 1678), p. 72 (hereafter referred to as *New Relation*). This edition has been used because its contemporary and very picturesque English more nearly approximates the original than a modern translation could. See also Jean-Claude Flachat, *Observations sur le commerce et sur les arts de l'Europe, de l'Asie, de l'Afrique, et même des Indes orientales, 1740–1758* (Lyons, 1766), II, 185 ff.; *Palais de Top Qapu*, p. 25.

4. Harvard MS, fol. 136.

5. *Edebiyat-i Osmaniyeh Mejmuasi*, Feb. 4, 1913.

6. Bobovi also wrote a treatise on Islam, *Tractatus* . . . *de Turcarum liturgia*, and a Turkish grammar and lexicon, and he translated the English Catechism and the Bible into Turkish. Both the original writings and the translations had a curious history. With the exception of the *Serai Enderum*, published in 1667, none of his works appear to have been published prior to his death, which, according to Cornelius Magnus, took place in 1672 (*Quanto di piu Curioso Turchi*, Sixth Letter, dated Oct. 14, 1672). Several were later resurrected and for a time enjoyed a not inconsiderable vogue. Between 1691 and 1767 there were two editions of the Latin translation of the *Tractatus* and two of an English translation, both annotated. With the exception

of the Gospel of St. Matthew, which was published in 1682, his translation of the Bible remained unpublished until 1819, between which date and 1853 it was revised and published in numerous editions both as a whole and in separate books — very possibly as a result of the Protestant missionary movement in the Near East which was begun about that time. By correspondence with the "Loco-Director" of the University of Leyden, V. F. Büchner, it has been possible to ascertain that the MS of Bobovi's translation of the Bible into Turkish, now in the possession of the university (Cov. Warnerianus, 390), was held, by the late Professor de Goeje, a well-known orientalist and author of the *Catalogue of Oriental Manuscripts of the Library of the University of Leyden*, as also by the Loco-Director, to be, in large part, an autograph manuscript of the translator. A marginal note appended at the end of the Gospel of St. John states that the translation was completed "Anno. 1644, ratione, oratione et enaratione [*sic*] Alberti Bobovu Leopo, litani Mercedem aeternam sperantis [*sic*]." As the result of the comparison of a facsimile of this signature with that on fol. 144 of Harl. MS 3409 of the British Museum, expert opinion of the Oriental Department of the same institution agrees with that of Dr. Woods of the Manuscript Section, that the Harleian manuscript is not in the handwriting of Bobovi.

7. The respective situations of these two halls as given in Plan III is confirmed by von Hammer (*Staatsverfassung*, pp. 29, 183), while Reimers and Murhard put them in reverse order (H. von Reimers, F. Murhard, *et al.*, "Ansichten von Konstantinopel und dem Kaiserlichen Serail," *Konstantinopel und St. Petersburg: der Orient und der Norden*, St. Petersburg, 1805–1806), II, 165.

8. Harvard MS, fol. 93.

9. *Ibid.*, fols. 35, 41–43, 63.

10. *Serai Enderum* [*sic*], trans. N. Brenner (Vienna, 1667), p. 42.

11. In the French version of the *Serai Enderum*, in which the key to the plan of the Great Hall is given, but not the plan itself, nos. 5 and 6 are designated as Stalls Polluted with Fleas; no. 10 as the Stall of the Sciences; no. 11, the Stall Polluted with Bedbugs; no. 14, the Stall of Musicians; and no. 15, the Stall of the First Assistant of the Head Usher (Bash Khalfa) (Harvard MS, fols. 100–107).

12. M^{xxx} d'Ohsson, *Tableau général de l'empire ottoman* (Paris, 1787–1820), III, 300, hereafter referred to as *Tableau général*.

13. According to Mehmed Refik Bey, formerly curator of the Grand Seraglio, these halls were rebuilt about 1270 or 1271 A.H. (1853/5).

14. Flachat, *op. cit.*, II, 179.

15. *New Relation*, p. 67; palace tradition.

16. The general plan of all the halls is said to have been the same (Harvard MS, fol. 107).

17. *New Relation*, chap. XV.

18. For location of these offices, see Flachat, *op. cit.*, II, 185, 195.

19. Pétis de La Croix, *État général de l'empire ottoman, depuis sa fondation jusqu'à présent, et l'abrégé des vies des empereurs, par un solitaire Turc, traduit en français* (Paris, 1695), I, 340 ff., hereafter referred to as *État général*.

20. *New Relation*, pp. 73–74.

21. *Ibid.*, p. 70.

22. *Ibid.*, pp. 66–67. Flachat, describing the Hall of the Treasury in the eighteenth century, mentions also an upper gallery and two wide, slightly elevated platforms at either side of the room, each of which, he says, could accommodate fifty beds (*op. cit.*, II, 187).

23. Palace tradition; *Palais de Topkapu*, pp. 23–24.

24. Flachat says: "One passes from the *Seferli Oda* into a bath" (*op. cit.*, II, 180).

25. *Staatsverfassung*, pp. 12 ff.

26. Pierre Gilles, *Antiquities*, p. 39; Flachat, *op. cit.*, II, 185.

27. Abd ur-Rahman Sherif Efendi, "Top Qapu Sarayi Humayunu," *Tarikh-i Osmani Enjumeni Mejmuasi*, no. VII. He mentions also a second apartment of the head treasurer underneath the Imperial Treasury, dated 1152 A.H. (1739/40).

28. *Histoire*, X, 194; Harvard MS, fol. 44.

29. Andrea Badoaro, *Relazione*, ser. III, vol. I, p. 360; *New Relation*, p. 66; *Tarikh-i Ata*, p. 12.

30. *New Relation*, p. 69; *Narrative of Travels*, I, 50.

31. According to Bobovi, the attendants in the bath were pages from the Great and Small halls and from the Hall of the Expeditionary Force (Harvard MS, fol. 21); according to Tavernier, who, it will be recalled, received his information from a page and an officer of the Imperial Treasury, they were pages from the Hall of the Treasury (*New Relation*, p. 36).

32. Harvard MS, fol. 28; *New Relation*, pp. 40–44; *Konstantinopel*, II, 181–184.

33. Harvard MS, fol. 28. Vigenère puts the number at two hundred (*op. cit.*, p. 61).

34. *Konstantinopel und St. Petersburg*, II.

35. *New Relation*, p. 43.

36. Harvard MS, fol. 28.

37. Palace tradition; see also *Tableau général*, III, 300.

38. *Top Qapu*, no. VII.

CHAPTER III

1. See Notes, Chap. I, n. 13, above.

2. L'Abbé Joseph de La Porte, *Almanach turc* (Paris, 1762), pp. 178–179.

3. *Ibid.*, p. 178; Giovio, *Histoire*, pp. I iii ff.

4. Guillaume Postel, *De la république des Turcs* (Poitiers, 1560), pt. III, p. 21.

5. *Histoire*, III, 167.

6. Adolphus Slade, *Travels in Turkey* (New York, 1854), p. 104, quoted by a Diplomatist [George Young], in *Nationalism and War in the Near East* (Oxford, 1915), p. 36.

7. Cited by A. H. Lybyer, *The Government of the Ottoman Empire* (Cambridge, 1913), p. 40.

8. Wratislaw, *Adventures*, trans. A. H. Wratislaw (London, 1862), p. 54.

9. The Mainotes inhabited a district of the Peloponnesus. According to Bobovi, Armenians as a race were exempt from military service "because their religion more nearly approaches that of the Nestorians, which the Turks esteem to be the purest type of Christianity" (Harvard MS, fol. 49). On the other hand, Knolles says that the tribute boys were not recruited from Asia because they were not of a sufficiently high quality (Richard Knolles, *Generall Historie of the Turkes*, London, 1687, pp. 984–985, quoted by Lybyer, *op. cit.*, p. 52).

10. Djevad Bey, *État militaire ottoman* (Constantinople, 1882), pp. 241, 250.

11. J. H. Mordtmann, "Devshirme," *Encyclopaedia of Islam*, I, 952–953; IV, 943.

12. J(ean) de Chavigny, *Discours parénétique sur les choses turques* (Lyons, 1606), pp. 2, 4; Christophe Richer, *Des coustumes et manières de vivre des Turcs* (Paris, 1540), p. ii; *La Généalogie du Grand Turc* (Paris, 1569), chap. X. To the contrary, d'Ohsson (*Tableau général*, III, 37–38) says one-fifth. See also Spandouyn, *Petit Traicté*, p. 59.

13. Chavigny, *op. cit.*, pp. 2, 4; Richer, *op. cit.*, pp. 11–12. The mangonel was a military engine used for throwing stones and javelins.

14. Djevad Bey, *op. cit.*, pp. 26, 27.

15. Akeska and Zozerum were in, or near, Circassia (Habesci, *État actuel*, p. 172). See also Harvard MS, fol. 49; *New Relation*, p. 9; Leopold von Ranke, *The Ottoman and the Spanish Empires*, p. 14; Lybyer, *op. cit.*, pp. 51–52.

16. Ali Riza Bey, "Saray Adetleri," *Sabah* (Constantinople, 1927/8).

17. The registers of the customhouse of Constantinople, cited by Tavernier, *New Relation*, p. 2.

18. See Chap. I, p. 38, above.

19. Spandouyn, *op. cit.*, pp. 59, 63; *Histoire*, X, 192.

20. Lybyer, *op. cit.*, p. 74. In addition to the authorities cited by Professor Lybyer, see also Nicholas de Nicholay, *Discours et histoire véritable des navi-*

NOTES TO CHAPTER III 201

gations, pérégrinations et voyages faicts en la Turquie (Antwerp, 1586, pp. 61–62; F. Antoine Geuffroy, *Briefve description de la court du grant Turc* (1541), in *Recueil de voyages et de documents, pour servir à l'histoire de la géographie depuis le XIII siècle*, ed. C. Schefer and H. Cordier (Paris, 1887), VIII, 230; Jean Chesneau, "Le Voyage de Monsieur Aramon, Ambassadeur pour Le Roy en Levant (1547)," in *Recueil de voyages*, VIII, 39. John Sanderson places the number from eight to nine hundred (*Sundry the personall Voyages, 1584–1602)*, in *Purchas His Pilgrims* (London, 1625), vol. II, lib. IX, pp. 1614–1640.

21. *Histoire*, X, 194. Geuffroy (*op. cit.*, p. 44) and Junis Bey (quoted, Lybyer, *op. cit.*, Appendix IV, p. 269) say that there were three hundred pages in the palace of Adrianople and four hundred in that of Galata; Postel (*op. cit.*, p. 20), that there were six to seven hundred; Chesneau (*op. cit.*, p. 40), three to four hundred; and Baudier (*Histoire généralle*, p. 17), four hundred in the *Saray* of Ibrahim Pasha. Evliya Efendi, whose numbers are usually much exaggerated, says that the *Saray* of Ibrahim Pasha had two thousand pages and ranked next to the Grand Seraglio in size (*op. cit.*, I, 175).

22. H. Marsh, *A New Survey of the Turkish Empire* (London, 1664), p. 112; Habesci, *État actuel*, pp. 157–187. Tavernier sets the number at only six hundred (*op. cit.*, p. 9).

23. *Relazione*, ser. III, vol. III, p. 264.

24. Mehemet Khalifeh, as quoted by Mehmed Refiq Bey, *Edebiyat-i Osmaniyeh Mejmuasi*, Feb. 4, 1913.

25. Hafiz Elias Bey, *Letaifi Enderun*, p. 216; *Tableau général*, III, 299–300.

26. Menavino says that the pages were admitted at fifteen years of age (*Trattato*, p. 91). Junis Bey (cited, Lybyer, *op. cit.*, Appendix II, p. 263), Ramberti (*ibid.*, Appendix I, p. 244), and Geuffroy (*op. cit.*, p. 230) agree upon eight years as the age of admission. Bobovi (Harvard MS, fol. 49) places it at ten years; Rycaut (*Present State*, p. 40), from ten to twelve years; Tavernier (*New Relation*, p. 2), from nine to ten; and Withers (in J. Greaves, *Miscellaneous Tracts*, II, 653), from twelve to fourteen.

27. Mehmed Refiq Bey, in *Edebiyati Osmaniyeh Mejmuasi*, Feb. 4, 1913; Habesci, *op. cit.*, I, 161.

28. The history of the word *ajemi-oghlanlar* shows an interesting evolution. Originally meaning a Persian (from Ajemistan, Persia), it came to be applied to all non-Arabian peoples; hence the derived meaning of a foreigner, or barbarian, and from that, an untrained one, or apprentice.

29. Baudier, *op. cit.*, p. 110; *Present State*, p. 42; *New Relation*, p. 9; Ahmed Rasim, *Resimli*. As to the military status of the *ajemi-oghlanlar*,

Ahmed Djevad Bey writes: "Although the gatekeepers and gardeners and other servitors attached to the palace were considered as forming part of the *Capou-Koulis*, or Imperial Guard, in reality they were only the servitors and guardians of the gardens. They accompanied the sultan upon the theater of war, but they had no function in the army. Their services were limited to being the guardians and servitors of the person of the sultan. They should therefore not be considered a part of the regular army" (*op. cit.*, p. 17).

30. Menavino, *op. cit.*, p. 91; Geuffroy, *op. cit.*, p. 242; Ahmed Rasim, *op. cit.*

31. Harvard MS, fol. 7; *Staatsverfassung*, p. 30; *Histoire*, X, 192.

32. Bon, *Il serraglio*, p. 35; *Present State*, pp. 26–27; *Tarikh-i Ata.*

33. *Present State*, p. 26; *Tableau général*, III, 299.

34. Menavino, *op. cit.*, pp. 5–12.

35. *Narrative of Travels*, I, 132 f. The time which Evliya gives as necessary for repeating the whole of the Koran, seven or eight hours, is, according to Professor Hitti, underestimated. For explanation as to the identity of the deceased Musa, see Notes, Chap. V, n. 63, below. Evliya completed the course of the Palace School in about three years, and after graduation entered the cavalry service and set out with Murad IV on his Persian campaign. Upon his return he was employed upon several diplomatic and financial missions, after which he became an independent traveler, for forty-one years roaming over different parts of Europe, Asia, and Africa. The voluminous narrative of his travels, which he spent the last ten years of his life in writing, is one of the classics of Turkish literature. Although Evliya is given to exaggeration in figures, particularly where it is a question of his own glorification or that of the Turkish race — he says, for example, that there were 366 towers and 12,000 battlements in the walls of the Grand Seraglio, 20,000 cypresses, 100,000 fruit trees, *et cetera*, in its gardens, and 40,000 souls within its walls — his work is a very valuable mirror of seventeenth-century life in "the countries of the eighteen monarchs where he visited," and an intensely human document.

36. For other instances of reward, see Postel, *op. cit.*, pp. 10–11; *Tarikh-i Ata.*

37. Geuffroy, *op. cit.*, p. 229; *Illustrations*, p. 53; Harvard MS, fols. 14–15; *Present State*, p. 37; *État général*, p. 138; *New Relation*, p. 6.

38. Bon, *op. cit.*, p. 41; Withers, *op. cit.*, p. 696.

39. Angiolello, *Historia*, fols. 50 ff.; *Histoire*, III, 317–318; Ahmed Rasim, *op. cit.*

40. Spandouyn, *op. cit.*, p. 63; Junis Bey, in Lybyer, *op. cit.*, Appendix II, p. 269.

41. *Histoire*, X, 279.

42. *Present State,* p. 37; Harvard MS, fol. 20.

43. Habesci, *op. cit.*, I, 160, 169–172.

44. *Tableau général,* III, 302; Hafiz Elias, *op. cit.*

45. Harvard MS; Du Loir, *Voyages,* p. 89.

46. *Konstantinopel und St. Petersburg,* II, 165–166.

47. Angiolello, *op. cit.*, fols. 50¹–50²; *Histoire,* III, 317–318; Vigenère, *Illustrations,* p. 53; Chesneau, *op. cit.*, p. 40; Du Loir, *op. cit.*, p. 89; *Staatsverwaltung,* p. 29.

48. Harvard MS, fols. 14–18; *Present State,* pp. 36–37; *Tableau général,* III, 300–303. On the other hand Tavernier (*New Relation,* p. 6) ranks the palace chamberlain after the heads of the Treasury and Commissariat.

49. "Qanun-name-yi ... Muhammad Khan," *Tarikh-i Osmani Enjumeni Mejmuasi,* no. III, supplement 13; Harvard MS, fols. 12, 18; *New Relation,* p. 66; *Histoire,* X, 193–194; *Staatsverwaltung,* pp. 26–27.

50. *Tarikh-i Ata.*

51. *Present State,* p. 36; Harvard MS, fol. 12; *New Relation,* p. 7; *Staatsverwaltung,* pp. 28–29; *Konstantinopel und St. Petersburg,* II, 165; Ahmed Rasim, *op. cit.* Although the first officers of the halls were occasionally pages, as a rule this office was held by white eunuchs.

52. Mehmed Refiq Bey, in *Edebiyati Osmaniyeh Mejmuasi,* Feb. 4, 1913.

53. Harvard MS, fols. 145–148.

54. Mehmed Refiq Bey, in *Edebiyati Osmaniyeh Mejmuasi,* Feb. 4, 1913.

55. *Staatsverfassung,* pp. 465–467; Harvard MS, fols. 13, 91–93.

56. A *lala* has been defined as "that indisputable personage in every old Turkish household, for which no English or no European equivalent can exist, for it arose from roots wholly foreign to them, wholly Oriental. The *lala* was the natural outcome of the marked separation between the indoor and outdoor life of that day and world. Indoors was the delicately intimate rule of women; out of doors was the realm of men. They could play there their proper role of protector, and one felt happy and secure in their presence. As child, and child only, one could share to the full the freedom of the two worlds, and one's *lala* was the natural companion in all the open-air places of experience. Then too he brings with him into memory that *je ne sais quoi* of the old-world service — devotion, attachment, pride, possession even — which the modern Turkish world has forgotten but which made so much of the warmth and color of the old household life. In the *lala's* strength one was secure; on his devotion one could rely tyrannously and from his innocent familiarity one could learn the truths and fables which only fall from the lips of primitive affection." (Halideh Edib, *Memoirs,* New York and London, n. d., pp. 6, 7.)

57. Ramberti, in Lybyer, *op. cit.*, Appendix I, p. 244; Junis Bey, *ibid.*,

Appendix II, p. 264; Geuffroy, *op. cit.*, p. 230; Navagero, *Relazione*, ser. III, vol. III, p. 43; *Illustrations*, p. 62; Harvard MS, fol. 60; Ahmed Rasim, *op. cit.*

58. Hafiz Elias Bey, *op. cit.*, pp. 387–389.

59. Harvard MS, fols. 85, 99–100.

60. *Ibid.*, fol. 20.

61. Menavino, *op. cit.*, p. 93; *Illustrations*, pp. 56, 62.

62. Harvard MS, fols. 18, 20; *Tableau général*, III, 299.

63. *Illustrations*, pp. 56, 62.

64. *Narrative of Travels*, I, 138; *Tarikh-i Ata*.

65. Harvard MS, fols. 20, 92; *Tarikh-i Ata*; von Ranke, *op. cit.*, p. 15.

66. *Illustrations*, p. 56.

67. *Menavino, op. cit.*, p. 94; *Tarikh-i Ata*.

CHAPTER IV

1. Menavino, *Trattato*, p. 91.

2. Abbate Giambatista Toderini, *Letteratura turchesca* (Venice, 1787), I, 85. There is also a French translation by M. l'Abbé de Cournand, *De la littérature des Turcs* (Paris, 1789).

3. Habesci, *État actuel*, I, 173–174; Dr. Hu Shih, *The Chinese Renaissance* (Chicago, 1933), pp. 6–16.

4. Habesci, *op. cit.*, I, 177; Harvard MS, fol. 20; *Staatsverwaltung*, pp. 13–30.

5. *Present State*, p. 32; *Histoire*, VI, 184 ff.

6. Toderini, *op. cit.*, I, 99–117.

7. *Histoire*, VI, 7, 184–185; Eugen Oberhummer, *Konstantinopel unter Sultan Suleiman dem Grossen* (Munich, 1902), pp. 22–24; Tafel XXII.

8. *Present State*, p. 27.

9. Djevad Bey, *État Militaire*, p. 74.

10. Nicholay, *Discourse*, pp. 3, 5.

11. In a statement to the author.

12. Spandouyn, *Petit Traicté*, pp. 179–180.

13. Angiolello, *Historia*, fols. 48–50; Baudier, preface, pp. 41–42.

14. Angiolello, *op. cit.*, fol. 49.

15. *Narrative of Travels*, pp. 1, 2, 188.

16. Sandys, *Travailes: Containing a History of the Original and Present State of the Turkish Empire* (London, 1658), p. 57.

17. Ogier Ghiselin de Busbecq, "Exclamatio: sive De re militari contra Turcam instituenda consilium," etc., in *Augerii Gislenii Busbecquii Omnia quae extant* (Pest, 1758), pp. 262–263, cited Lybyer, p. 74.

18. Flachat, *Observations*, II, 188 ff.; Richer, *Des coustumes*, p. 11.

19. *Narrative of Travels*, I, 132 ff.; *Tarikh-a Ata*.

20. Flachat, *op. cit.*, II, 188 ff.

21. Busbecq, *Life and Letters*, trans. C. T. Forster and F. H. B. Daniell (London, 1881), I, 154–155.

22. N. N. Law, *Promotion of Learning*, pp. 54–55, 63.

23. Menavino, *op. cit.*, p. 94; Harvard MS, fol. 65; *Illustrations*, p. 56; Ahmed Rasim, *Resimli*; *Present State*, p. 26.

24. *Present State*, p. 26.

25. *Konstantinopel und St. Petersburg*, II, 145–146.

26. Harvard MS; *Present State*, p. 32; *Narrative of Travels*, I, 132–139.

27. Toderini, *op. cit.*, 77–78.

28. Bon, *Il serraglio*, p. 36; *Konstantinopel und St. Petersburg*, II, 145 f. See also *Present State*, p. 31; Harvard MS.

29. Harvard MS.

30. *Present State*, p. 31.

31. *Ibid.*, p. 31.

32. Wilhelm Pertsch, *Die arabischen Handschriften der Bibliothek* (Gotha, 1878–92), no. 194, 2, d–c–b.

33. Carl Brockelmann, *Geschichte der arabischen Litteratur* (Weimar, 1898–1902), II, 21.

34. *Ibid.*, I, 304, n. 13; II, 207, n. 11.

35. *Ibid.*, II, 713, n. 430.

36. *Ibid.*, II, 214.

37. *Ibid.*, II, 432.

38. *Ibid.*, I, 378.

39. *Ibid.*, I, 174.

40. *Ibid.*, I, 376.

41. Harvard MS; *Present State*, p. 31.

42. *Present State*, p. 31.

43. Gibb, *History of Ottoman Poetry*, IV, 176, n. 3; 257–258, n. 2.

44. Brockelmann, *op. cit.*, I, 453; Edward G. Browne, *Literary History of Persia* (London, 1902–1906), II, 115.

45. Habesci, *op. cit.*, II, 177.

46. Harvard MS.

47. Rashid Efendi, as quoted by Toderini, *op. cit.*, II, 37–41. At the time that Toderini caused the catalogue of the Seraglio library to be made, he was convinced that there were two separate collections of books in the palace, one of Arabic, Persian, and Turkish books and MSS, and a second of Greek, Latin, Syrian, etc., but it is not clear whether the latter collection still remained in the Treasury, where it had formerly been stored, or whether, as

Rashid Efendi asserts, it had actually been removed to the library, in the center of the third court, remaining under lock and key in the original cases. His statement is as follows: "the page who made the Catalogue for me told me, moreover, that an enormous number of books in Greek and Latin, etc., existed, but that these were in the Treasury. Then to be sure that the Page had told me the truth, I questioned with great adroitness the Venetian Dragoman, a high personage among the Turks who had been the custodian of the Imperial Library of the Seraglio, about this information and he affirmed emphatically that there were really Arabic, Persian and Turkish books and that the catalogue of these was not very different from that of the Library of Santa Sophia, but that the codices were better written and more elegantly bound and that there were several hundred more of these than at Santa Sophia. He also affirmed that there were really Greek, Latin and Syrian books locked up in cases [in the Treasury?] and that there was a rumor that among these were several codices which had been brought from Jerusalem. We can, therefore, affirm that there are really codices in Greek, Latin and other languages in the Seraglio. . . . All these volumes bear the imprint of the great seal or 'black letter' [*tughra?*] which proves that they belong to the Imperial Library. This Imperial Library is paved with marble and the walls also are faced with precious oriental marbles. On one side the books are placed in closed cupboards, the doors of which are made of fine brass and real crystal, and all around the walls are divans. A man from Georgia who has several compatriots in the Seraglio said that he had entered the Library at least nine times, which fact was confirmed by Ismail Bey" (Toderini, *op. cit.*, II, 45–49).

48. The existence of this list is mentioned by James Dallaway, *Constantinople, Ancient and Modern, with Excursions to the Shores and Islands of the Archipelago and to the Troad* (London, 1797), p. 23, n. 1.

49. It would seem not to have been beyond the realm of possibility at the time that the Abbate Toderini visited Constantinople to obtain access to the inner library of the Grand Seraglio. Gustav Flügel gives an account of a certain "C— who in 1718–1719 was said to have examined the books of this library, i.e., the library founded by Sultan Ahmed III, as it seems. It is another than that founded by Mustafa III in the outer part of the palace in 1767, and Toderini calls the former (the one C— examined), the Inner (Library), not the Outer Library, as Hammer-Purgstall holds" (*Lexicon bibliographicum et encyclopaedicum*, London, 1855–58, p. 389). See also Sir Edwin Pears for a further account of scholars allowed to examine the MSS of the Imperial Library (*Turkey and Its People*, London, n. d., p. 129).

50. Toderini, *op. cit.*, II, 52–54. The complete catalogue is given in Italian (*ibid.*, II, 53–88) and in Turkish script (as an appendix, unpaged, in the same

volume). Professor D. Adolf Deissmann of the University of Berlin, who had access to the Seraglio library in 1931 and later published a descriptive list of the non-Islamic works, is of the opinion, in the light of Muhammad's tastes and interests as described by Critoboulos, that certain works, in particular two manuscripts of the Geography of Ptolemy (Codex Seragliensis, no. 27, 14/15th century and Codex Seragliensis, no. 57, 13th century), formed part of the original collection of Muhammad II (*Forschungen und Funde im Serai*, Berlin and Leipzig, 1933). Herr Emil Jacobs, who in 1919 published an account of the library based on early sources (*Heidelberger Akademie der Wissenschaften. Sitzungsberichte der Heidelberger Akademie der Wissenschaften. Philosophisch-historische Klasse*, Heidelberg, vol. X [1919]), had no first-hand knowledge of the library.

51. Henry George Farmer, *Arabian Influence on Musical Theory* (London, 1925), pp. 62–64; Arnold and Guillaume, *The Legacy of Islam* (Oxford, 1931), pp. 368 ff.

52. Harvard MS.

53. Toderini, *op. cit.*, I, 222–223.

54. Harvard MS.

55. Toderini, *op. cit.*, I, 223–225; Farmer, *op. cit.*, pp. 83–96, 272.

56. Toderini, *op. cit.*, I, 228.

57. *Ibid.*, I, 236.

58. Pietro della Valle, *Viaggi descritti da lui medesimo in lettre familiari all' erudito suo amico Mario Schipano* (Venice, 1661–63). The edition here referred is the French translation, *Voyages en Turquie, Egypt, Palestine, Perse, Indes orientales, Chypre, et autres lieux* (Paris, 1745), I, 87–88.

59. T. Kowalski, "Ottoman Turkish Literature" in *Encyclopaedia of Islam*, IV, 972–973.

60. Toderini explains this statement more fully as follows: "The character and theory of Turkish music may be made clear by comparison with our European music. Our [octave] comprises twelve semitones, the Turkish twenty-four, since each European tone is divided into four intervals by the Turkish masters. . . . These minute intervals [i.e., quarter-tones], although not used in our music, are very essential to theirs. Devoid of harmony, being always sounded at the unison, Turkish music compensates by a great melodic variety and richness of ornamentation" (*op. cit.*, I, 243–244, 247).

61. Henry George Farmer, *Turkish Musical Instruments in the Seventeenth Century as described in the Siyahat Nama of Evliya Chelebi* (Glasgow, 1937), identifies the above instruments as follows, the transliteration in each instance following that of the author: *kemenchah*, viol with hemispherical sound chest (pp. 43–44); *santur*, dulcimer which has metal strings and is played with little wands (p. 34); on the other hand, the psaltery, with which

Bobovi identifies it, has gut strings, and is plucked; *musiqal,* Panpipes (p. 22); *nay,* flute (p. 18); *ud,* lute (p. 41); *tanbur,* the two- or three-stringed pandore (pp. 35–36); *chaghaneh,* classified under "Rattles," as the Jingling Johnny, or Chapeau Chinois, an instrument that was borrowed from the Turks by European military bands in the eighteenth century (p. 10); *chugur,* the five-stringed pandore of the Janizaries (pp. 39–40); *buru,* horn or trumpet (pp. 28–31); *davul,* ordinary drum (pp. 17–18); *naqara,* small kettledrum (pp. 14–15); *dunbalek,* general term for kettledrum (pp. 16–17); *zil,* cymbal, which was a "noteworthy instrument" (p. 9). See also *Narrative of Travels,* II, 225–240.

62. *Tarikh-i Ata.*

63. Toderini says of the military band of the Grand Seraglio: "The sultan's band of Turkish musicians is a truly magnificent affair, playing these instruments for the two *Bairams,* for festival occasions, for court ceremonies, and at the sultan's will. They all play in unison, some at the upper and lower octaves, as is the character of Turkish music" (*op. cit.,* I, 239). According to Farmer (*Turkish Musical Instruments in the Seventeenth Century,* p. 7), the band "played a military *nubat* of three parts twice daily." The *nubat* is defined by Redhouse as "each one of five times a day, corresponding more or less with the hours of prayer, when formerly the band of eastern music used to be played in the courtyard of governors" (J. W. Redhouse, *Turkish Dictionary,* London, 1880, p. 844).

64. *Illustrations,* p. 62; Harvard MS; Toderini, *op. cit.,* p. 233; Djevad Bey, *op. cit.,* pp. 237–241.

65. Habesci, *op. cit.,* I, 178.

66. *Ibid.,* I, 74.

67. *New Relation,* p. 41.

68. This was a hard, swift game, played with the intention of "striking mortally." It took place, usually preceding the wrestling matches, in the open space in front of the Kiushk of Tiles (*Chinili Kiushk*) or near the Kiushk of Pearls (*Indjili Kiushk*). It was especially popular in the latter part of the eighteenth century, as attested by the fact that the sultans were nearly always present at noontime.

69. A dervish, reported to have been a companion of Haji Bektash, who was renowned in legend as a slayer of dragons and giants (F. W. Hasluck, *Christianity and Islam under the Sultans,* vol. II, chap. XXXII).

70. Harvard MS, fols. 140–141.

71. Ernest Mamboury, *Constantinople: Tourist Guide* (Galata, 1925), p. 406; Karl Wulzinger, *Baudenkmaler zu Konstantinopel* (Hanover, 1925), p. 5. Antoine-Ignace Melling's map of Seraglio Point shows the "Place et Bâtiment du Dgirid" (*Voyage pittoresque de Constantinople et des rives du*

Bosphore, Paris, 1807–24); and that of Abd ur-Rahman Sherif Efendi, the target stones and target positions for archery practice in the same field ("Top Qapu Sarayi Humayuni," *Tarikh-i Osmani Enjumeni Mejmuasi,* VI). E. W. Lane gives an interesting description of *jerid* as it is played by the peasants of upper Egypt (*Manners and Customs of the Modern Egyptians,* Paisley & London, 1895, pp. 362–363).

72. William Harborne, Public Record Office: *State Papers, Foreign: Turkey,* vol. I, Entry, Pera, July 21, 1582.

73. *Present State,* p. 28.

74. Hafiz Elias Bey, *op. cit.,* pp. 389–390.

75. *Present State,* p. 28.

76. Bon, *op. cit.,* p. 37; Baudier, *Histoire,* p. 109; *Present State,* p. 28; *New Relation,* p. 69; Harvard MS, fol. 79.

CHAPTER V

1. Harvard MS, fols. 44–48; *Tableau général,* III, 299; *État général,* I, 388–389; Habesci, *État actuel,* I, 162; *New Relation,* p. 8; *Histoire,* X, 192; Joseph Eugène Beauvoisins, *Notice sur la cour du Grand Signor* (Paris, 1809), pp. 28–29; *Staatsverwaltung,* pp. 29–30; Geuffroy, in Schefer and Cordier, *Recueil des voyages,* VIII, 244.

2. Angiolello (*Historia,* fol. 19), Navagero (*Relazione,* ser. III, vol. I, p. 44) and Vigenère (*Illustrations,* pp. 59–60) say that promotions were usually made every two years; and Gianfranc Morosini (*Relazione,* ser. III, vol. III, p. 264), every three years.

3. *Tarikh-i Ata.*

4. Harvard MS, fol. 21; *Present State,* pp. 27, 28; *Histoire,* X, 196.

5. *Trattato,* p. 125; Garzoni, *Relazione,* ser. III, vol. I, p. 394.

6. Harvard MS; *Present State,* pp. 17, 27. In the "Fragment of an Account of an Insurrection at Constantinople, 1651" (Brit. Mus., Harl. 7021, fol. 425), the anonymous author of which claims to have been a page of the Great Hall, the number is said to have been six hundred.

7. *Staatsverwaltung,* pp. 229–230. Pétis de La Croix, writing about the same time, puts the number at five hundred (*État général,* I, 389).

8. Navagero, *Relazione,* ser. III, vol. I, p. 42.

9. *Illustrations,* pp. 30, 58. On the other hand, Sir Paul Rycaut says that the two schools were of the same rank (*Present State,* p. 27), and the three following authorities agree that the daily allowance of the pages of both halls was the same; Harvard MS, fols. 44, 64; Pétis de La Croix, *Mémoires,* I, 133–148; *Staatsverfassung,* pp. 29–30.

10. Harvard MS, fols. 31, 36; Ahmed Rasim, *op. cit.*

11. Baudier, *Histoire*, p. 114; *New Relation*, p. 36; Mehmed Refiq Bey, *Edebiyat-i Osmaniyeh Mejmuasi*, Feb. 4, 1913.

12. *Present State*, p. 27.

13. *Tarikh-i Ata*.

14. Ahmed Rasim, *Resimli*.

15. Baudier, *op. cit.*, p. 114; *Present State*, p. 27; *New Relation*, p. 36.

16. Menavino, *Trattato*, p. 12; Navagero, *Relazione*, ser. III, vol. I, p. 44; *Present State*, p. 27; *New Relation*, p. 36; *Illustrations*, pp. 52, 56–58; *Tableau général*, III, 299. Menavino's statement that the pages were not encouraged to write Turkish perfectly would seem to be disproved by the nature of certain of the positions to which they were appointed upon departure from the Palace School.

17. Bon, *Il serraglio*, p. 35. Bobovi makes no mention of instruction in the use of arms in the preparatory schools. Among second-hand sources there is considerable contradiction as to the stage at which physical exercises began. Vigenère says that running, jumping, fencing, and archery began in the "large chamber" (*Illustrations*, p. 52); Baudier, that the first physical exercises began in the "second chamber" and riding in the "third" (*op. cit.*, p. 115). Navagero (*Relazione*, ser. III, vol. I, pp. 42–45), and Tavernier (*New Relation*, p. 36) make no mention of physical exercises before the halls of the Commissariat and Treasury.

18. Harvard MS, fol. 20; *New Relation*, p. 37; Pétis de La Croix, *Mémoires du Sieur de La Croix* (Paris, 1684), I, 142; *État général*, I, 389; *Konstantinopel und St. Petersburg*, II, 168.

19. Harvard MS, fols. 138–139; *Present State*, p. 28; *Tableau général*, III, 295; *Konstantinopel und St. Petersburg*, II, 168; Ahmed Rasim, *op. cit.*

20. Harvard MS, fols. 138–139; *New Relation*, p. 71.

21. See differential table of pages' allowances, Chap. IV, pp. 102–103, above.

22. Withers, in John Greaves, *Miscellaneous Tracts*, II, 671, 673–674; Harvard MS; Beauvoisins, *op. cit.*, pp. 30–31.

23. Hafiz Elias Bey, *Letaifi Enderun*, pp. 260–261.

24. Spandouyn, *Petit Traicté*, p. 62; Harvard MS; *Staatsverwaltung*, pp. 55–57; Lybyer, *Government of the Ottoman Empire*, p. 129, n. 3. According to the Comte de Choiseul-Gouffier, the *Baltajis* were originally a corps of eight thousand who accompanied the sultan on all excursions (*Le Voyage pittoresque de la Grèce* (Paris, 1782–1822), II, 480.

25. Menavino, *op. cit.*, pp. 91 ff.; *New Relation*, p. 36.

26. *New Relation*, p. 66; *Narrative of Travels*, I, 49; *Tarikh-i Ata*.

27. Menavino, *op. cit.*, pp. 91–94; Badoaro, in Alberi, *Relazione*, ser. III, vol. I, p. 360; Harvard MS, fols. 9, 27; *Tarikh-i Ata*, II, 446. The two Chamlijas are hills on the Asiatic side of the Bosphorus.

28. Angiolello, *op. cit.*, fol. 50². Ali Efendi estimates the number to have been thirty.

29. Figures for the reign of Suleiman, as given by Hezarfen Hussein, *Staatsverfassung*, p. 96.

30. Hezarfen Hussein, cited in *Staatsverfassung*, p. 96; Harvard MS, fol. 27; *New Relation*, p. 65; *État général*, I, 390; *Histoire*, X, 192; Pétis de La Croix, *Mémoires*, I, 133–148.

31. *New Relation*, pp. 65–66; *Tableau général*, III, 295; *Histoire*, X, 193–194; Ahmed Rasim, *op. cit.*

32. *Tarikh-i Ata*, I, 172.

33. *Narrative of Travels*, I, 51.

34. *New Relation*, pp. 65–66.

35. Bon, *op. cit.*, p. 42; Withers, *op. cit.*, II, 696.

36. *New Relation*, pp. 45–51.

37. Du Loir, *Voyages*, p. 80; Hezarfen Hussein, as quoted in *Staatsverfassung*, p. 86; Harvard MS, fols. 90, 100; *Histoire*, X, 192.

38. Navagero, *Relazione*, ser. II, vol. I, p. 45; Ali Efendi, *op. cit.*; *New Relation*, p. 5; von Hammer estimates the number to have been forty (*Histoire*, X, 194).

39. *Present State*, p. 36; *New Relation*, p. 7.

40. *New Relation*, p. 74.

41. *Ibid.*, pp. 48–49.

42. *Ibid.*, p. 49; Hafiz Elias, *op. cit.*, p. 244.

43. Harvard MS, fol. 24.

44. *Ibid.*, fol. 24; *New Relation*, p. 35; Ahmed Rasim, *op. cit.*

45. *New Relation*, pp. 52–53.

46. *Top Qapu*, no. VII.

47. Angiolello, *op. cit.*, fol. 50²; *Staatsverfassung*, p. 96; "Qanun-name-yi . . . Sultan Muhammad Khan," *Tarikh-i Osmani Enjumeni Mejmuasi*. In addition to the thirty-two pages as decreed by law, there were also three officers.

48. Menavino does not mention the pages of the royal chamber as such, but says that there was a first officer of the royal bedchamber, fifteen valets, and thirty-five *odalandari* (*oghlanlari*) who had charge of the wardrobe and served the meals of the sultan (Menavino, *op. cit.*, p. 91); Ramberti, that there were six pages who served the royal person (in Lybyer, *op. cit.*, Appendix I, p. 243); Chesneau, that there were twenty-five (in Schefer, *Recueil de voyages*, VIII, 39); Navagero, that there were twenty-five to thirty (*Relazione*, ser. III, vol. I, p. 42); and Postel, that while there were commonly twelve, there were sometimes only eight or ten (*op. cit.*, p. 23).

49. Du Loir, *op. cit.*, pp. 91–93; Harvard MS, fol. 33; *Present State*,

p. 28; *New Relation*, p. 7; Pétis de La Croix, *Mémoires*, I, 139–140; Ali Efendi, *Kunh al-Akhbar*; *Tableau général*, III, 295.

50. *Staatsverwaltung*, pp. 22–23. According to Djevad Bey, *op. cit.*, p. 33, the *Boluks* had the privilege of guarding the Holy Standard.

51. Hafiz Elias Bey, *op. cit.*

52. Bon, *op. cit.*, p. 37; John Greaves, *Miscellaneous Tracts*, II, 674–675.

53. Menavino, *op. cit.*, p. 95.

54. See differential table of pages' allowances, Chap. IV, pp. 102–103; also Bon, *op. cit.*, p. 37.

55. Bon, *op. cit.*, p. 37. Habesci, who gives the number of officers of the royal bedchamber as fifteen, says that nine of these were masters of petitions, and that it was the remaining six who were sent upon messages to pashas and tributary sovereigns (*État actuel*, I, 175–176).

56. *New Relation*, p. 37; Ahmed Rasim, *op. cit.*

57. *Staatsverwaltung*, p. 16.

58. Ali Efendi, *op. cit.*

59. Geuffroy, *op. cit.*, pp. 227–228; Postel, *De la république des Turcs*, p. 5. The latter mentions a ewer-bearer, but not a cup-bearer.

60. Harvard MS, fol. 116 ff. This list is virtually the same as those given by d'Ohsson, *Tableau général*, III, 295, and by von Hammer, *Histoire*, X, 196. On the other hand Bon enumerates only fourteen officers (*op. cit.*, p. 37), von Hammer, twelve (*Staatsverwaltung*, II, 15), and Habesci, fifteen (*op. cit.*, I, 175).

61. Harvard MS, fol. 136; *Present State*, p. 29. Habesci puts the number of masters of petitions at nine (*op. cit.*, I, 175–176); and von Hammer, at fifty-five: the forty pages of the royal bedchamber; the first four officers of each of the other three upper chambers; and the first three officers of the court, the chief white Eunuch, the prefect of the palace, and the first officer of the royal bedchamber (*Staatsverwaltung*, p. 59).

62. *Tableau général*, III, 295; Mehmed Refiq Bey, in *Edebiyat-i Osmaniyeh Mejmuasi*, Feb. 4, 1913. A reception suite in the *selamlik*.

63. A young Armenian who was first a page in Galata Saray and later in the Great Hall. Shortly after his transfer to the Grand Seraglio, he was made sword-bearer to Murad IV (Harvard MS).

64. *Narrative of Travels*, I, 133–138.

CHAPTER VI

1. Bon, *Il serraglio*, p. 35; Menavino, *Trattato*, pp. 102–103; Du Loir, *Voyages*, pp. 71–73; *New Relation*, pp. 35–37; Ahmed Rasim, *Resimli*.

2. Angiolello, *Historia*, fol. 50²; Menavino, *op. cit.*, pp. 102–103; Harvard MS, fol. 40.

3. Bon, *op. cit.*, p. 37.

4. *Present State*, p. 29; Baudier, *Histoire généralle*, p. 111. Menavino's statement (*Trattato*, p. 21), that the pages of the commissariat always accompanied the sultan, refers to a period prior to the establishment of the Expeditionary Force; and that of d'Ohsson (*Tableau général*, III, 300 ff.), to the effect that the sword bearer supported a lodging and harem in the city, to a late period when the system of government by a slave class had disintegrated.

5. Harvard MS, fol. 3; *New Relation*, p. 68; *Staatsverwaltung*, pp. 29–30.

6. Harvard MS, fol. 34. *Tarikh-i Ata*.

7. Thomas Dallam, "Diary of Master Thomas Dallam (1599–1600)," *Early Voyages and Travels in the Levant*, Hakluyt Society, LXXXVII (London, 1893), 62–63.

8. Menavino, *op. cit.*, p. 94.

9. Harvard MS, fol. 22.

10. *Ibid.*, fol. 34, 78; Ahmed Rasim, *op. cit.*

11. This account of the school life is taken largely from Harvard MS, fols. 37, 75 ff.; *Tableau général*, III, 300, 303; *Tarikh-i Ata*; Mehmed Refiq Bey, *Edebiyat-i Osmaniyeh Mejmuasi*, Feb. 4, 1913.

12. Harvard MS, fols. 82–83.

13. *New Relation*, p. 22; *Konstantinopel und St. Petersburg*, I, 28.

14. Menavino, *op. cit.*, pp. 101–102.

15. Harvard MS, fol. 64.

16. *Tarikh-i Ata*; Ahmed Rasim, *op. cit.*

17. *New Relation*, p. 36.

18. Menavino, *op. cit.*, p. 103; Postel, *De la république des Turcs*, pt. III, pp. 3, 11.

19. Bon, *op. cit.*, p. 39; Withers, in John Greaves, *Miscellaneous Tracts*, II, 653; Harvard MS; Du Loir, *op. cit.*, pp. 91–93; *Present State*, p. 30.

20. *Tableau général*, III, 300 ff.

21. *Present State*, p. 30; Habesci, *État actuel*, I, 176.

22. Menavino, *op. cit.*, pp. 103–104; Navagero, *Relazione*, ser. III, vol. I, p. 44; *Illustrations*, pp. 59–60; Harvard MS.

23. *Present State*, p. 50.

24. Bon, *op. cit.*, p. 39; Pétis de La Croix, *Mémoires*, I, 393 f.

25. Harvard MS, fols. 35–36; *Illustrations*, pp. 59–60.

26. *Present State*, p. 30; Navagero, *Relazione*, ser. III, vol. I, p. 44. John Greaves, *Miscellaneous Tracts, Letters, Poems, etc.* (London, 1736–37), II, 683, says that the grand vizir entertained the pages for three or four days until they were provided with houses of their own.

27. Postel, *op. cit.*, p. 19.

28. The career of Ali Pasha, as worked out in detail by Professor Lybyer, was as follows:

"Ali Pasha was a native of Dalmatia. Levied with the tribute boys, he was admitted to the principal palace at a time when Ibrahim Pasha was *Odabashi*, or head of the Inner Chamber of pages. In the course of time he was made *Kapuji*, or gatekeeper. When Ibrahim became grand vizier, Ali became *Chasnejir*, or chief taster, to Suleiman, and held that office during the expedition to Vienna in 1529. In due course he was discharged from the palace, and appointed to high office outside. He soon reached the grade of *Agha*, or general of the *Ghurebas*, the lowest of the four divisions of the regular cavalry, and was then promoted to be *Agha* of the *Spahi-oghlans*, the highest of the cavalry divisions. Next he became second equerry and later first equerry (*Emir-al-akhor*), then *Agha* of the Janissaries, then *Beylerbey* of Rumelia. In the last capacity he attended the sultan in the Persian war of 1548–1549. As a reward for special services in the war he was made pasha of Egypt in 1549, and at the time of his departure was nominated vizier. Returning to Constantinople in 1553, he was made third vizier, and upon the death of Rustem in 1561, he became grand vizier. Because of jealousies and enmities caused by his promotions he had hardly a friend left; nevertheless, he was able to hold the favor of Suleiman until his death in 1565" (*Government of the Ottoman Empire*, pp. 87–88).

29. *New Relation*, p. 8; *Histoire*, X, 195; Lybyer, *op. cit.*, p. 103. Mouradja d'Ohsson says that originally it was the pages from the royal bedchamber who were made head gatekeepers (*Tableau général*, III, 301).

30. A. Heidborn, *Droit public et administratif de l'empire ottoman* (Vienna-Leipzig, 1909–12), I, 145; *Present State*, bk. II, chap. VI.

31. Lybyer, *op. cit.*, pp. 98, 99.

32. *Present State*, pp. 185, 187, 186.

33. Giovio, *Histoire*, I iii–I iiii. This account seems to be the basis of that by C. Richer, *Des Coustumes et manières de vivre des Turcs*, published two years later (Paris, 1540), p. 14.

34. Busbecq, *op. cit.*, I, 283–284.

35. Spandouyn, *Petit Traicté*, p. 62; Harvard MS, fol. 34.

36. Bon, *op. cit.*, p. 39; Withers, in J. Greaves, *Miscellaneous Tracts*, II, 674; *Present State*, p. 29.

37. "Qanun-name-yi . . . Sultan Muhammad Khan," *Tarikh-i Osmani Enjumeni Mejmuasi*, no. III, supplement 13.

38. *Tableau général*, III, 300 ff.; Ahmed Rasim, *op. cit.*

39. *Present State*, p. 193.

40. *Staatsverfassung*, p. 96.

41. Menavino, *op. cit.*, p. 104; Sancy, "Correspondance de Turquie" (Bibl. nat., fonds fr. 7095), fol. 98 f.; Bon, *op. cit.*, p. 40; Harvard MS, fols. 3, 9.

CHAPTER VII

1. As quoted by Lybyer, *Government of the Ottoman Empire*, p. 44.

2. *Nationalism and War in the Near East* by a Diplomatist (London and New York, n. d.), p. 35.

3. Djevad Bey, *État militaire*, pp. 77, 78.

4. *Relazione*, ser. III, vol. III, p. 389, trans. Lybyer, *op. cit.*, p. 43.

5. Bon, *Il serraglio*, p. 35; Baudier, *Histoire générale*, p. 113; Withers, in J. Greaves, *Miscellaneous Tracts*, II, 666; *New Relation*, p. 2; *Tarikh-i Ata*, I, 94 ff.

6. Pietro della Valle, *Viaggi descritti*, I, 108.

7. *Staatsverwaltung*, pp. 29–30.

8. *État général*, I, 388.

9. Djevad Bey, *op. cit.*, pp. 252–254.

10. Habesci, *État actuel*, I, 163.

11. Ahmed Rasim, *Resimli*.

12. F. Giese, "Das Seniorat im osmanischen Herrscherhause," *Mitteilungen zur osmanischen Geschichte* (Hanover, 1926), II, 248–256.

13. Public Record Office: *State Papers, Foreign: Turkey*, vol. I, entry July 19, 1582. This MS is torn in places.

14. Harvard MS, fols. 44–48; *Histoire*, X, 192–197; *Tableau général*, III, 299.

15. Harvard MS, fol. 44–46.

16. *Tableau général*, III, 294–295, 299–300. As Bobovi (1665) and Sir Paul Rycaut (1670) describe all six schools of the Grand Seraglio as still in existence, it is possible that the Great and Small halls were closed, not in 1651, the year of the death of Kiusem Sultan, but after Muhammad IV attained his majority. On the other hand, Tavernier (1675) mentions only four halls: the Small Hall and the halls of the Commissariat, Treasury, and Royal Bedchamber. Beauvoisins, writing in 1809, says that after the abolishment of the Great and Small halls the Galata Saray remained the only preparatory school (*Notice*, p. 31). Habesci in 1784 and Hafiz Elias in 1822 mention only three halls, those of the Royal Bedchamber, Treasury, and Commissariat, with from four to five hundred students.

17. Hafiz Elias Bey, *Letaifi Enderun*, pp. 88–89.

18. *Tableau général*, III, 301.

19. *Ibid.*, p. 249.

20. *Ibid.*, pp. 492–494.

21. J. Reid, *Turkey and the Turks* (London, 1840), pp. 261–265; Mrs. J. E. Blunt, *The People of Turkey* (London, 1878), chap. XXX.

INDEX

INDEX

Abbasid caliphs, 14, 188

Abd al-Latif, 25

Abd ul-Aziz, Sultan, 73

Abd ul-Hamid II, 98

Abd ul-Mejid, Sultan, 57, 63, 64, 132, 182

Abd ur-Rahman Sherif Efendi, 64, 107

Abubequer el Tortuxi, 19

Adrianople school, 22, 23, 43, 44, 79, 80, 126, 174, 178

Ahmad b. Muhammad al-Quduri, 109

Ahmad b. Muhammad al-Shaznawi, 109

Ahmed I, 44, 47, 74, 98, 131, 173

Ahmed III, 43, 68 f., 110, 132, 168

Ahmed Pasha, 23

Akbar the Great, 19

Ali Agha Hazretleri, Devletlu, 181

Ali Bey, see Bobovi, Albert

Ali Efendi, 40, 196

Ali Pasha, 163, 213 f.

Ali Qushji, 26

Aliens assimilated as pages, 8, 21, 75 f., 130

Allowances, see under Pages

Alp Arslan, 12

Amir Bukhari, 22

Amyrutzes, Georges, 34, 35

Angiolello, Giovanni Maria, 25, 32, 35, 37, 39, 40, 42, 102, 152

Appointments of pages, 163–170; high offices, 168 f.; Imperial Guard, 163, 168; pensions, 169; *Sipahis*, 164 f.

Arabic language, *see under* Curriculum of the Palace School

Archery, *see under* Curriculum of the Palace School

Army, recruited from European provinces, 75. *See also* Janizary corps; *Sipahis*

Ashariyah, 12, 16

Ata Bey, Tayyar Zadeh Mehmed, vii, 7, 8, 32, 37, 39, 187

Auxiliary schools, 43 f., 79 f., 85, 126

Avicenna, 110

Baidawi, 108

Barbaro, Marcantonio, 74

Bassano da Zara, Luigi, 45

Bath of Selim II, 45 f., 51, 54, 63, 66 f., 124

Baudier, Michel, 5

Bayazid I, 22, 77

Bayazid II, 29, 36, 41–43, 79, 83, 92, 194, 196

Bayazid, son of Suleiman I, 167

Bayrams, 30, 85, 116, 118, 122, 124, 157, 178

Baysunghur, 25

Bellano, Bartolomeo, 36

Bellini, Gentile, 35, 36, 42

Berchem, Max von, 14, 16

Berlinghieri, Francesco, 36

Bobovi, Albert (Ali Bey), 47 f., 50, 64, 102, 108, 113–115, 117, 153, 157, 159, 197 f.

Bon, Ottaviano, 5, 124

Books in the Palace School and the Library, 108–111, 205 f.

Brenner, Nicholas, 48

Buildings of the Palace School, *see* Plan of the buildings

Bukhari, 109

Burhan ad-Din Ali al-Marghinani, 109

Busbecq, Ogier Ghiselin de, 98, 100, 167

THE *Middle East* COLLECTION

Arno Press

Abbott, Nabia. **Aishah:** The Beloved of Mohammed. 1942

Addison, Charles G. **Damascus and Palmyra.** 1838. 2 Vols. in 1

[Adivar], Halidé Edib. **Turkey Faces West.** 1930

Baddeley, John F. **The Rugged Flanks of Caucasus.** 1940. 2 Vols. in 1

Barker, Edward B. B., ed. **Syria and Egypt Under the Last Five Sultans of Turkey.** 1876. 2 Vols. in 1

Bell, Gertrude Lowthian. **Syria:** The Desert & The Sown. 1919

Bowring, John. **Report on the Commercial Statistics of Syria.** 1840

Brydges, Harford Jones. **The Dynasty of the Kajars.** 1833

Churchill, [Charles H.] **The Druzes and the Maronites Under the Turkish Rule from 1840 to 1860.** 1862

Denon, Vivant. **Travels in Upper and Lower Egypt.** 1803. 3 Vols. in 1

Donaldson, Bess Allen. **The Wild Rue:** A Study of Muhammadan Magic and Folklore in Iran. 1938

Eton, W[illiam]. **A Survey of the Turkish Empire.** 1798

Forbes-Leith, F. A. C. **Checkmate:** Fighting Tradition in Central Persia. 1927

Fraser, James Baillie. **Narrative of the Residence of the Persian Princes in London, in 1835 and 1836.** 1838. 2 Vols. in 1

Fraser, James Baillie. **A Winter's Journey (Tâtar) from Constantinople to Tehran.** 1838. 2 Vols. in 1

Gobineau, Joseph Arthur. **Romances of the East.** 1878

Islamic Taxation: Two Studies. 1973

Kinneir, John Macdonald. **A Geographical Memoir of the Persian Empire.** 1813

Krusinski, J[udasz Tadeusz]. **History of the Late Revolution in Persia.** 1740. 2 Vols. in 1

Lane-Poole, Stanley. **Cairo:** Sketches of Its History, Monuments, and Social Life. 1898

Le Strange, G[uy], ed. **Don Juan of Persia:** A Shi'ah Catholic, 1560-1604. 1926

Leeder, S. H. **Modern Sons of the Pharaohs:** A Study of the Manners and Customs of the Copts of Egypt. 1918

Midhat Bey, Ali Haydar. **The Life of Midhat Pasha.** 1903

Miller, Barnette. **The Palace School of Muhammad the Conqueror.** 1941

Millspaugh, A[rthur] C[hester]. **The American Task in Persia.** 1925

Naima. **Annals of the Turkish Empire from 1591 to 1659 of the Christian Era.** 1832

Pasha, Djemal. **Memories of a Turkish Statesman, 1913-1919.** 1922

Pears, Edwin. **Life of Abdul Hamid.** 1917

Philby, H[arry] St. J[ohn Bridger]. **Arabia of the Wahhabis.** 1928

St. John, Bayle. **Village Life in Egypt.** 1852. 2 Vols. in 1

Sheil, Lady [Mary]. **Glimpses of Life and Manners in Persia.** 1856

Skrine, Francis Henry and Edward Denison Ross. **The Heart of Asia:** A History of Russian Turkestan and the Central Asian Khanates from the Earliest Times. 1899

Sykes, Mark. **The Caliphs' Last Heritage:** A Short History of the Turkish Empire. 1915

Sykes, P[ercy] M., ed. **The Glory of the Shia World.** 1910

De Tott, Baron. **Memoirs of Baron de Tott.** 1785. 2 Vols. in 1

Ubicini, M. A. **Letters on Turkey.** 1856. 2 Vols. in 1

Vambery, Arminius. **Arminius Vambery:** His Life and Adventures. 1914

Vambery, Arminius. **History of Bokhara.** 1873

Waring, Edward Scott. **A Tour of Sheeraz by the Route of Kazroon and Feerozabad.** 1807